E DUE

The Administration
Of United States Foreign
Policy Through the
United Nations

The Administration Of United States Foreign Policy Through the United Nations

By
DONALD G. BISHOP

Edited by
Gerard J. Mangone

1967
Oceana Publications, Inc.
Dobbs Ferry, New York

The Maxwell School Series on the Administration of Foreign Policy Through the United Nations

Editor

GERARD J. MANGONE

1. *The United Kingdom* by Rosalyn Higgins

2. *The United States* by Donald G. Bishop

Table of Contents

Appendices

vii

Foreword

This is the second of a series of studies on the administration of foreign policy through the United Nations by various governments in the contemporary international system. The purpose is to analyze the commitment of several states to the United Nations system and to examine in detail the organization of their executive agencies and legislatures in response to the needs of modern multilateral diplomacy.

The experience of most governments with international organizations has been brief compared to the historic development of ministries of foreign affairs, resident embassies, bilateral negotiations, and treaties, yet today the United Nations is the meeting place of 122 nations, with nearly all the great issues of peacekeeping, economic and social cooperation, or human rights brought into its councils, commissions, and committees. For the scholar and the statesmen it is of more than academic interest to understand the ways in which governments handle contemporary international issues through the United Nations system with details about their administrative practices that inevitably affect policy decisions.

Dr. Donald G. Bishop, Professor of Political Science at the Maxwell School of Citizenship and Public Affairs, spent several months in Washington and New York studying the administration of United States foreign policy through the United Nations and interviewing many officials both in the Department of State and the United

States Mission to the United Nations. In this book he examines the support that the American people have given to the United Nations and describes the Bureau of International Organization Affairs in the Department of State, which has primary responsibility for the conduct of foreign affairs under the President. Furthermore, he outlines the problems of American diplomatic delegations to the United Nations and the role of the United States Permanent Mission in New York with its exercise of "corridor diplomacy". Dr. Bishop vividly illustrates the complexity of international relations for the American government and how many agencies other than the State Department, engage in negotiations and agreements on matters of national security, health, education, labor, commerce, agriculture, and so forth, which lead to difficulties in coordinating foreign policy. Finally, the part played by the American Congress in United Nations affairs, especially in the annual delegations to the General Assembly, is discussed and some conclusions are drawn about future United States-United Nations relationships.

The manuscript for this book was originally presented at the Second Maxwell Institute on the United Nations in August 1965 at the Villa Serbelloni of the Rockefeller Foundation at Bellagio, Italy. Twenty members of the Institute, all with academic or government experience in United Nations affairs, read and discussed Dr. Bishop's work, which was then substantially revised in 1966 and finally edited at the Maxwell School of Syracuse University.

GERARD J. MANGONE

1

American Support of the United Nations

Although the United States never joined the League of Nations, the vision of Woodrow Wilson remained alive, like a sign going on before those wandering in the wilderness of isolationism. Nothing in the domestic politics of the United States tarnished this vision even though the decisions taken in 1920 on American membership in the League could not be reversed. The failure of the League to prevent war in the 1930's was interpreted by many Americans as a failure of this specific organization or of its leading members, but not of the idea itself, and those Americans were spurred on to a greater effort to produce a more perfect international organization that might succeed where the League had failed.

During World War II, accordingly , a group worked in the Department of State, under the leadership of Leo Pasvolsky, on plans for a new postwar international organization to maintain peace and security, and the United

1

States was both host and major participant in the 1944 Dumbarton Oaks conference where the specific plans for the United Nations were discussed by the Great Powers. At the Yalta Conference in 1945, Franklin D. Roosevelt negotiated with the Soviet Union and the United Kingdom to resolve crucial questions about the structure of the UN, and the United States again was host to the San Francisco Conference where the final Charter was signed. Later the American government ratified the treaty with the overwhelming support of the Senate and encouraged the location of the UN in the United States so that in the fullest physical and psychological sense America became a leader in this new hope for world peace.

American enthusiasm for the UN has been so widespread and intense that it has invited disillusion. Many Americans appeared to believe that the millenium had arrived and that peace was now firmly established for all time, merely because of the existence of the UN, although others had a more realistic attitude and attempted to demonstrate the difficulties of the new system as well as its hopes. A large number of citizens' organizations, such as the American Association for the United Nations (now the United Nations Association of the United States of America) , and the Foreign Policy Association with its associated World Affairs Councils, have conducted a widespread educational effort about the UN, and United Nations Day has became almost a national holiday in the United States, celebrated with festivities in every corner of the country. Hundreds of colleges and thousands of public schools introduced the study of international organizations into their curricula. Surely no international organization has ever been the center of so much public attention.

The UN, moreover, is today an important news center, with the radio and television networks and the press associations stationing reporters and crews at UN headquarters. In a crisis, such as the Korean aggression in 1950 or the U. S.-Soviet confrontation over Cuba in 1962, the eyes of the American television audience have been focused on the Security Council or the General Assembly to a degree unforeseen by those who wrote the Charter. The UN headquarters in New York has become a leading tourist attraction, and even when there are no political crises it has become increasingly difficult to obtain tickets to the visitors' galleries as millions of Americans have sought to understand something about the UN.

Every President, beginning with Harry S. Truman, who assured the first General Assembly on October 23, 1946 that the policy of the United States would be to "support the United Nations with all the resources we possess . . . not as a temporary expedient but as a permanent partnership,"[1] has frequently expressed the American government's support of the UN. With the post World War II divisions between the Communist bloc and the West, the United States quickly emerged in the Security Council as a leader of the democratic nations in the UN and the international organization became a field on which many of the diplomatic battles of the Cold War were fought.

American interest in the UN has been both idealistic and realistic. The United States, for example, has supported the UN peacekeeping activities, believing that they can provide a peaceful way of achieving the kind of world which the American people seek. Against aggression in 1950 in Korea, what purported to be a UN action was to a very complete degree an American action, and the

---

[1] *The United States and the United Nations,* Report by the President to Congress for the Year 1946. Washington, Government Printing Office, 1947, p.iii.

American government was, accordingly, willing to provide the great bulk of manpower, supplies, money, and military leadership for the undertaking. After Korea, under other UN arrangements, every peacekeeping operation of the UN from Egypt to the Congo to Cyprus had the support of the United States, which has contributed the major share of the needed funds. And although the United States attempted to shift more responsibility for peacekeeping to the General Assembly where it felt it had a better influence on the outcome, it yielded to the consensus of the General Assembly in 1965 not to force the Soviet Union and other states to pay for peacekeeping expenses as assessments or lose their vote.

In the same area of security matters are questions of disarmament. Here, too, the United States has maintained a great interest in UN action, beginning with the establishment of the UN Atomic Energy Commission in 1946 and the meetings wherein the United States representative, Bernard Baruch, proposed the establishment of an international atomic energy development agency and set forth a plan to end the fears generated by the spectre of atomic weapons controlled by national governments. Since then the United States, through a number of widely discussed schemes and proposals, has endeavored to bring about disarmament under multilateral auspices, but without much success.

In the field of human rights, the American government has also believed that the UN could fill a very useful role, especially through its distinguished delegate Eleanor Roosevelt, who was for several years the best-known member of the UN bodies that hammered out a Universal Declaration of Human Rights and then sought to proceed to a legally-enforceable Covenant of Human Rights. Finally, the United States has been a generous supporter of the whole gamut of UN economic and social activities, as will be shown in its contributions, both through the Organization itself and the specialized agencies.

A balanced appraisal of United States participation in the UN system must indicate, however, that the United States has not supported the UN at every point and to the fullest degree. If the United States agreed to UN involvement in certain important Cold War crises—as in Greece, Korea, Hungary, and Cuba—there was no similar action at other times. One of the most dangerous post-war crises involved Germany and the Berlin question, but the UN was involved in this only very indirectly and almost accidentally. Two major Asian problems, Taiwan with the offshore Chinese islands, and Indochina, have never been inscribed on the UN agenda, and Viet Nam only at a very late stage.

In some of these situations, the United States was opposed to referral to the UN, and in others the UN was merely bypassed. With respect to disarmament, while the Soviet government bears much responsibility for the failure of the UN to make progress, the United States has also slowed action by careful reference to its national policy and its insistence on on-site inspections. Moreover, if the United States can claim much credit for the Declaration of Human Rights, it is also true that American opposition to certain provisions in the draft Covenant of Human Rights reduced the international progress which was possible. The UN Genocide Convention, submitted to the United States Senate in 1949, has never been ratified by the American government. While the United States has posed as one of the strongest supporters of the International Court of Justice and the general concept of world law, strong American reservations were made to the compulsory jurisdiction provisions of the Statute and the government, despite pressure from many groups throughout the country, has steadfastly refused to weaken these reservations to demonstrate its confidence in the Court. And although the United States has been a leader of the democratic world, it was the 94th member of the United Nations, the last of those required under the Charter, to approve the Charter amendments of 1965 that enabled an enlarged membership of the Organization to have greater representation on the Security Council and the Economic and Social Council (ECOSOC).

Some observers, therefore, have seen the United States as a "fair weather friend" rather than a "permanent partner," supporting the UN when American interests could be served, but bypassing it and weakening it when American interests might be curbed by UN action. The American government, like other governments, must protect its national interests, and its idealism and philanthropy have been limited by the fear of succumbing to a rival power. The attacks of American officials against the Soviet government for the extreme measures taken in the UN to protect Russian sovereignty, might be turned from time to time against the United States itself. Nevertheless, United States support for the UN has been very substantial.

Contributions. One of the best evidences of American support for the United Nations has been the amount and nature of the financial contributions made by the American government. The UN depends upon two types of revenue: (1) the assessments levied upon member-states by the General Assembly, and (2) "voluntary" contributions, the amount of which each member determines for itself, taking into account its national interests in such special programs as economic development or scientific cooperation.

The United States government's assessment in the early years of the UN was approximately 40% of the regular UN budget. By stages this has been reduced to 32%, with the American government claiming that it had no objection to the amount of the contributions, but that it did not believe it psychologically wise for any member to pay more than one-third of the costs of any international organization. It is expected that the American share will be reduced to 30% in the near future. The UN budget has increased in size so that, even with the United States paying a smaller proportion of the total, the American assessment increased from $13,841,000 in 1948 to $34,479,000 during fiscal year 1966 (the year ending June 30, 1966).

Each of the UN specialized agencies has its own budget, moreover, and its own scale of assessments. In 1948 the United States belonged to seven of these agencies and paid $8,369,000; in 1966 it belonged to nine and was assessed $33,725,000.

In the fall of 1966, the United States was expected to pledge $70,000,000 to the United Nations Development Programme, the program arising in January 1966 from the merger of the formerly separate Expanded Program of Technical Assistance (EPTA) and the Special Fund. The United States' pledge is subject to the limitation that it will not exceed 40% of the total contributions to UNDP.[1] This system of voluntary pledging has been used to bring pressure on other members to support UN programs, rather than to expect the United States to carry an "unduly large" share of the financial burden.

Meanwhile the UN became involved in an unanticipated number of peace-keeping activities requiring the United Nations Emergency Force (UNEF), the United Nations Operation in the Congo (UNOC), and the United Nations Force in Cyprus (UNFICYP). Assessments for these operations have not been accepted by many states and contributions have been uneven. The United States has made voluntary contributions in addi-

---

[1] United States. House of Representatives. *Foreign Assistance and Related Agencies Appropriations Bill, 1967*. House Report No. 2045. 89th Congress, Second Session. 1966. p. 15.

tion to assessments levied for UNEF. In the first two years of UNEF, for example, the American assessment was $13,000,000 while the American government voluntarily contributed another $14,000,000, a total of 49.34% of the cost.

In fiscal 1967, the anticipated United States' assessment for the regular UN budget and its specialized agencies totalled $73,296,00 and, adding in voluntary contributions to special UN programs, the total United States contribution to the UN system amounted to $217,849,000, as follows:

Regular UN Budget	$32,793,000
Specialized Agencies	40,503,000
Voluntary Peacekeeping Contributions	16,838,000
Special Voluntary Programs	137,715,000
	$217,849,00 [2]

If the United States has contributed $158,000,000 a year to the UN, which is the average for the period just cited, it has done so in the belief that American interests have been advanced by the Organization. The members of Congress hardly make appropriations of this size for merely idealistic reasons. While Congress has been increasingly restive in recent years because certain UN members have refused to contribute to some of the most expensive of the UN programs, it has repeatedly yielded to the arguments of the Department of State that American national policies are advanced through UN programs and that to abandon the UN programs would only

---

[2] United States. House of Representatives. *Foreign Assistance and Related Agencies Appropriations Bill, 1967*. House Report No. 2045. 89th Congress, Second Session, 1966, p. 15 And, United States. House of Representatives. Hearings before a Subcommittee of the Committee on Appropriations. *Departments of State, Justice, Commerce, etc . . . for 1967*. 89th Congress, Second Session. 1966. pp. 486-8.

cost more in American efforts through unilateral programs. Although Congress has repeatedly urged reform
of UN financing, it has continued to pay far more than
the American assessed share of UN costs.

International Civil Servants Another index of United
States support of the UN is the number and kind of
American nationals who have been engaged as staff in
the secretariats of the Organization and its agencies.

When the League of Nations was organized, some ex-
ponents of international organization believed that each
government should attach some of its civil servants
temporarily to the Secretariat, while others believed that
individuals should be recruited by the League, hired,
paid, and directed by it, with no control exercised by
national governments. The second view was adopted and
in 1945 the United Nations embodied this principle in
Article 100 of the Charter.

Nevertheless, the role of the international civil servant
was not clearly understood. Some Americans thought
that if the United States paid a large share of the costs
of an international organization, it should have a pro-
portionate share of the staff. This was specifically stated
by one Congressman who discovered that there were only
fourteen Americans among the 390 employees of the
United Nations Educational, Scientific and Cultural Organization (UNESCO) when the United States was
paying nearly half of the cost. "We should have better
representation," he asserted.[3] This idea was resisted at
first, but it has been accepted more and more in recent
years by both the Department of State and the United
Nations. "There is an important political and also management reason for the U. S. Government taking much
more responsibility—as most other governments do for

[3] Dept. of State Appropriation Bill for 1948. Hearings before
the Subcommittee of the Committee on Appropriations, House
of Reps., 80th Cong., 1st Sess., Washington, 1947, p.862.

their nationals—for getting the right Americans into the right spots in the right international organizations. This is the direction in which we are moving."[4] If the annual conference of an international organization makes the broad policy decisions, the staff does the preparatory work and implements the resulting policy, which may be the more important part of the activity.

The following table shows the numbers and percentages of Americans employed in various types of international organizations and programs in February 1963, both in the total staff and the professional category.

TABLE I

	Total Staff	Total U.S.	U.S. %	Total Profsnl.	U.S. Profsnl.	U.S. %
UN — Regular Secretariat	5935	1376	23.2	1425	364	25.5
UN Programs	20170	217	1.1	1453	117	8.7
Subtotals	26105	1593	6.1	2878	481	16.7
Specialized Agencies	8790	945	10.7	3917	558	14.2
Technical Assistance	2776	277	10.0	2776	277	10.0
Inter-American Organizations	2095	510	24.3	900	274	30.4
Regional Organizations	2850	71	2.5	835	69	8.3
Other Internat'l Orgs.	919	94	10.2	349	57	16.3
Total	43535	3494	8.0	11655	1716	14.7

Source: Adapted from Report of Advisory Committee on International Organizations, Department of State, *Staffing International Organizations,* April 1963, pp.26-30.

---

[4] Hearings before a Subcommittee of the Committee on Appropriations, House of Reps., 88th Cong., 2nd Sess., Depts. of State, Justice, and Commerce [etc.], Appropriations for 1965, Washington, 1964, p. 750.

American participation has varied widely from agency to agency; for example, from .02% in the United Nations Relief and Works Agency for Palestine Refugees in the Near East (UNRWA) up to 40.54% in the Special Fund and 48.28% for the Technical Assistance Board; from 0 in the Universal Postal Union (UPU) to 37.8% in the International Bank for Reconstruction and Development (IBRD) and 43.3% in the International Monetary Fund (IMF). Although the nationals of the United States exceed the number of any other member of the UN itself, they are far from equal in percentage to the American contribution to the UN budget.

The United States government does not view Americans employed by international organizations as "instructed delegates." The question has not been one of having delegates to follow the bidding of the government, but of having staff members, loyal to the international organization, who would contribute, as part of their service, a sympathetic understanding of American views and American methods.

In the past, employment in international organizations has not attracted many highly skilled Americans, for several reasons. In the early years of the UN the United States government showed little concern about the number of its nationals employed by international organizations. Washington's weakness in protecting American employees of the UN against the political attacks of Senator Joseph McCarthy hardly encouraged other Americans to seek UN employment. Better salaries have been available in the United States, from private industry or even the American national government than in the UN system, while few Americans had the linguistic skills necessary for international work. There was no tradition in American history like that of certain European countries for international service and, up to recently, not many Americans were accustomed to working and living abroad. Finally, Executive Order 10422, January 9, 1953 required security clearance for Americans employed by international organizations, often involving two to six months, during which time there was no certainty of employment. Although a later executive order eased this problem for certain international employees, the waiting time was not shortened. When a House of Representatives committee visited Europe to study international organizations, the members found this to be a serious problem:

> The international organizations state that the effect . . . has been to make it very difficult to employ United States citizens in international organizations. Recruitment of United States citizens has been drastically curtailed . . . in some of the organizations it is practically nil. . . . Organizations are hiring persons of other nationalities who not only are not as competent but who probably involve a much greater risk as far as the interests of the United States are concerned.[5]

But the committee did not recommend an abandonment of this policy, which is still in effect.

In 1965 an official of one specialized agency said that "X", a candidate for employment had taken a job elsewhere in view of the delay in the security clearance process. The official stated that this was the last time he would consider an American for such employment; he could not, he said, afford to wait for United States clearance when other nationals were readily available. In one sense the American government is its own enemy and Congress must share responsibility for our not being "better represented."

Another problem has been the decentralization of recruiting. Recruiting for the UN itself is handled in the New York headquarters but each of three programs

---

[5] *Report of the Special Study Mission on International Organizations and Movements, . . .* of the Committee on Foreign Affairs, 83rd Congress, 2nd Sess., Union Calendar No. 473, House Report No. 1251, February 25, 1954, p.118.

and nine specialized agencies works separately. There is no uniform system of announcing or filling vacancies. At the American end, federal agencies with substantive interests in international organizations have operational responsibility for such recruiting. Thus the Department of Agriculture has liaison with the Food and Agriculture Organization (FAO), the Department of Labor with the International Labor Organization, (ILO), the Atomic Energy Commission (AEC) for the scientific side and the Department of State for the administrative side of the International Atomic Energy Agency (IAEA), and so on. What is left is lodged in the Department of State, but not all in one place since the Pan American Union and the Organization for European Cooperation and Development (OECD) are largely handled by the regional geographic bureaus. The International Recruiting Service (IRS), in the Office of International Administration of the Department of State until recently, was left to deal with the United Nations itself, UNESCO, EPTA, the International Telecommunication Union (ITU), and some other small organizations. In practice IRS locates about half of the candidates and the other agencies the other half.

In any case, IRS was not equipped to do the recruiting job. It has had no roster of the 3,500 Americans employed in international organizations. It had a card-file of those seeking employment but the cards had to be sorted by hand. When provision was made in 1964 for machine-sorting, there was no one to put the information on punch cards. Needing 700-1400 candidates a year, IRS had a total of three professional recruiters until 1963. As one Department official told a congressional committee, a job like that can't be done "with two men and a girl."

This type of recruiting, moreover, is complex and time-consuming. In one recent case, India sought a team of petroleum experts. IRS approached the Geological Survey, the American Petroleum Institute, the Society of Petroleum Engineers, and a number of American corporations and universities, but could find no suitable candidate. The Russians were sufficiently interested to offer to send interpreters if their nominees were chosen. The New York office of EPTA discovered a suitable American candidate, and in February 1965 the team was working in India with six Russians, one Czech, and one American, with three Russian interpreters paid by the Soviet government.

At a conference of the American Economic Association in 1965, the Agency for International Development (AID) used twenty-one recruiters to locate economists; IRS had two. Until recently IRS had a total of four recruiters; the British government has twenty-four for a population only one-fourth as large. A few governments can virtually require the service of their experts in international service while other governments find financial supplements to make international employment attractive. Both of these powers are beyond the American government. Almost every European country has a central office, a National Committee for Technical Assistance, to handle recruitment for UN technical assistance employees. The United States has no such committee.

The American government, however, is more interested in this problem than previously. One forward step came in 1958 with the passage of Public Law 85-795 which authorized the head of any federal agency to detail any employee to an international organization for a period up to three years. Any such employee is entitled to all rights and benefits for retirement, group life insurance, compensation, and annual leave, and to reemployment in his former (or an equal) position. Only modest use, however, has been made of this law. In six years 255 employees from eighteen federal agencies served in nineteen international organizations or an average of about forty a year.

The Advisory Committee on International Organizations created by the Department of State in 1962 studied this problem of staffing international organizations and concluded that:

> If the United States is fully to discharge its obligations, it must play a far more effective role than it has in the past in assisting the leadership in these organizations to meet their personnel requirements. We have therefore urged that our historic policy of political and financial backing for the United Nations should now be accompanied by a greatly strengthened program of assistance to the staffing effort.[6]

The Committee believed that a "laissez-faire" attitude which had developed in the United States should give way to a more positive attitude, and it called the government's activity in this sphere "hit or miss."

On the basis of its analysis, the Committee made a series of recommendations, including the following:

1. The President should announce a positive policy of assisting international organizations to recruit competent Americans.

2. The position of Special Assistant to the Assistant Secretary for International Organization Affairs should be created, to serve as a central information and record point and to coordinate the efforts of United States missions. Actual recruitment would remain decentralized.

3. Arrangements should be made to facilitate the cooperative use of recruiting mechanisms by AID, the State Department, and counterpart U. S. government agencies for multilateral aid.

---

[6] Report of the Advisory Committee on International Organizations, *op. cit.,* p.1.

4. Government agencies and private industry should be encouraged to release employees for international organization service.

President Johnson subsequently announced such a policy on August 16, 1964. An office of Special Assistant was created but has now become a part of the new Office of International Organization Recruitment. Foreign Service Officers have been encouraged to serve with international organizations. In September 1964 a Liaison Group for Staffing International Organizations was formed, consisting of representatives of twenty-nine federal agencies. One additional recruiter for IRS was appointed and an additional secretarial position filled. The chief of the recruiting unit made a first trip to Europe to visit UNESCO, FAO, and the World Health Organization (WHO), and an officer at the United States Mission to the United Nations (USUN) was assigned full-time to work on this problem. On June 7, 1966 Ambassador and Mrs. Arthur Goldberg, joined by Vice President Hubert Humphrey, gave a reception in New York for all United States citizens working at the UN, which was the first time an American Ambassador has evidenced the interest of his government in such a manner. There is general agreement that these developments are just a beginning and that much more needs to be done.

The attitude of the United States towards the UN, in sum, has been ambivalent and often inconsistent, but it is still true that the support provided by both the American government and the American public for the UN compares most favorably with that provided by any other member of the Organization. There is no doubt that American attitudes and policies have been very greatly internationalized in the past twenty years and the administrative machinery of the United States government reflects new and increasing participation in UN activities.

2

The Department of State and the United Nations

The executive branch of the United States government under the leadership of the President has great freedom in the area of foreign relations to initiate and execute policy. Congress, of course, passes laws and approves the budget as well as retaining an after-the-fact system of audit and criticism. Nevertheless, the Chief Executive has great discretion and independence in the field of foreign affairs. The President by necessity, must entrust much of the policy-making and day-to-day administration in international relations to the Department of State, Thus, an analysis of how the United States government maintains relations with the UN, and implements policy through the UN must begin with the structure of the Department of State in Washington. In the following simplified chart the key bureau for UN relations is the Bureau of International Organization Affairs (IO).

There are three main aspects of the organization and work of the department. First, the department has *geographic* bureaus for major areas of the world: African, European, Far Eastern, Near Eastern and South Asian, and Inter-American Affairs. Each of the regions is subdivided into countries and a "desk officer" is in charge of American relations with a single country. Secondly, since foreign affairs cannot always be divided geographically, the department also contains a series of *functional* bureaus, each of which deals with a topical part of foreign relations, such as Economic Affairs, Educational and Cultural Affairs, Intelligence and Research. Third, the Department has *administrative* offices for personnel training, finance, and so forth, the part which carries on important but often routine functions that make it possible for the rest of the department to work smoothly.

The Bureau of International Organization Affairs

It is not clear where the Bureau of International Organization Affairs (IO) belongs in the departmental structure. It is not a geographic bureau, for it is not concerned with a single region, but with the whole world. It is not a functional bureau, for its interest is not with a single topic, but with many. It is neither fish nor fowl, though it has some characteristics of both. It has been customary to place it on the departmental organization chart along with the geographic bureaus, but the 1965 *Congressional Directory* lists it with the functional bureaus. It does not fit into the old bilateral diplomatic pattern but is a new creation designed for a new situation.

Following World War II there was great concern about the ability of the United States government to fulfill its duties adequately in the face of new responsibilities. The study of the Department of State made by the 1949

Hoover Commission emphasized that there should be a "clear and unencumbered" line of command from the Secretary of State down to the lowest level. One important element was the fixing of responsibility for action in line units to deal with American relations with the rest of the world.

> Both the regional and international organization Assistant Secretaries would *at the action level* be responsible for and be equipped, in terms of personnel, to deal with not solely "political" aspects of foreign affairs, as is the basic conception of the duties of the existing geographic office directors, but for all aspects, whether they be political, economic, public opinion, intelligence, or administration.[7]

The Hoover Commission believed that the Assistant Secretary for International Organization Affairs should, so far as possible, obtain his policy guidance from the various regional units. Once it was accurate to say that IO lay astride, but not in the traditional mainstream of foreign policy. This description seems less accurate in the mid-1960's. The geographic bureaus still possess important controls over American foreign relations, but their power has somewhat diminished. It would seem that the Assistant Secretary for International Organization Affairs has indeed become "an additional agent in this field," to use the words of the Hoover Commission, and that, while he must carefully coordinate the activities of his bureau with those of the geographic bureaus he must on many occasions act on his own. It has also become necessary for the Assistant Secretary to handle many of the substantive policy matters that come from the various geographic bureaus affecting United States missions to international organizations without reference to the top command of the department. The bureau has developed

---

[7] *Report on the Organization of the Executive Branch of the Government,* by Hoover Commission. Copyright 1949. McGraw-Hill Book Company, p.161.

a degree of autonomy not foreseen by the Hoover Commission and has been divided into six offices:

Office of the Assistant Secretary. The Bureau of International Organization Affairs "provides guidance and support for United States participation in international organizations and conferences, and acts as the channel between the Federal Government and such organizations. It prepares United States positions on international organization matters, and coordinates the overall Federal Government interest with respect thereto."[8]

It is the duty of the Assistant Secretary to see that these functions are properly fulfilled. Congress has appropriated funds for forty-two permanent positions in the Assistant Secretary's office, which indicates something of the magnitude of the work. In the nomination of delegates to an international conference, this Office may be concerned only with seeing that dealines are met, but the duties normally involve much more than this. In the formulation and implementation of policies in the political and security field, the complete energy and talent of the whole office may be devoted to reviewing possible American policies with other members of the Department of State and a dozen other federal agencies.

The Assistant Secretary is responsible for all actions and activities of his segment of the department. As the focal point for the resolution of all disagreements within his jurisdiction which cannot be settled at a lower level, he represents his Bureau in the resolution of all difficulties which must be settled at the Assistant Secretary level or, failing this, appealed to the Under Secretary or the Secretary of State. He is also responsible for conducting relations with his counterparts in the Department, in other federal agencies, and in other governments.

---

[8] *United States Government Organization Manual,* 1963-64, Washington, Government Printing Office, p.82.

It is important, for example, that IO officers, including the Assistant Secretary, have first-hand knowledge of the political, economic and social matters with which this Bureau is concerned. Sometimes this can best be obtained by personal observation and by contact with officials of other governments or of international organizations. It has been estimated that there should be "at least five trips a year for such purposes, principally to Europe, where most of the international organizations are headquartered."[9]

The Assistant Secretary also has the legal responsibility of transmitting to our delegations to international conferences the final, approved position papers of the United States government and providing briefings to members of American missions to international organizations.

In 1961, the Assistant Secretary cogently indicated to a Congressional committee the factors in the growth and change of the UN system which had produced significant increase in the Bureau's workload:

1. The membership of the United Nations and its subsidiary agencies has grown rapidly and will continue to grow as other countries obtain their independence.
2. The United Nations is increasingly becoming an operating agency . . .
3. Economic and social operations of the United Nations and its related agencies are becoming a big business involving total expenditures of about $200,000,000 or more for next year and on which the United States puts up the largest portion and therefore must take the largest responsibility for policy leadership.[10]

---

[9] Hearings before a Subcommittee of the Committee on Appropriations, House of Representatives, 88th Congress, 2nd Session, Depts. of State, Justice and Commerce [etc.] Appropriations for 1965, p.277.

[10] Hearings before the Subcommittee of the Committee on Appropriations, House of Representatives, 87th Cong., 1st Sess. Depts. of State, Justice and Commerce [etc.] Appropriations, 1962, p.355.

ASSISTANT SECRETARY FOR INTERNATIONAL ORGANIZATION

INTERNATIONAL ORGANIZATION RECRUITMENT

Provides leadership and coordination of U.S. departments' and agencies efforts to help international organizations secure the services of highly qualified U.S. citizens from government and private life; analyzes and develops U.S. policy on personnel problems relating to international organizations.

OFFICES OF:

INTERNATIONAL CONFERENCES

Handles U.S. Government official participation in international conferences and activities stemming from U.S. multilateral negotiations and membership in intergovernment organizations. Administers "International Conferences and Contingencies Appropriations" for this purpose.

CONFERENCE ADMINISTRATION STAFF

CONFERENCE PROGRAM STAFF

UNITED NATIONS POLITICAL AFFAIRS

Plans, formulates and implements U.S. policies and positions, with advice or review of other areas of the Department, on political and security matters in the UN.

UNITED NATIONS POLITICAL AFFAIRS

INTERNATIONAL SECURITY AFFAIRS

GENERAL ASSEMBLY AND UN ORGANIZATION AFFAIRS

DEPENDENT AREA AFFAIRS

ORGANIZATION AFFAIRS

OCTOBER 1966

EXECUTIVE DIRECTOR

Insures that the Bureau, USUN and other missions which the Bureau backstops are properly organized and prepared to discharge their substantive responsibilities; coordinates and directs personnel and management functions and reviews budgetary questions involving the Bureau; serves as financial coordinator for appropriations administered by Bureau.

REFERENCE AND DOCUMENTS

MESSAGE CENTER

INTERNATIONAL ECONOMIC AND SOCIAL AFFAIRS

Plans, formulates and implements U.S. policies and positions, with advice or review of other areas of the Department on international aspects of economic, social, health, labor, scientific, human rights, freedom of information and technical assistance matters in the General Assembly, the Economic and Social Council and specialized agencies.

- INTERNATIONAL EDUCATION AND SOCIAL AFFAIRS
- ECOSOC AND GENERAL ASSEMBLY AFFAIRS
- INTERNATIONAL ECONOMIC AFFAIRS
- INTERNATIONAL HEALTH AFFAIRS
- INTERNATIONAL LABOR AFFAIRS
- INTERNATIONAL SCIENTIFIC ORGANIZATIONS

INTERNATIONAL ADMINISTRATION

Develops policy and proposals respecting financial support for international organizations, as well as general administration and management of such organizations. Reviews effectiveness of the management of international organizations and maintains controls on payments. Administers UN Headquarters Agreement. Formulates position on privileges and immunities of international organizations.

- SPECIALIZED AGENCIES AND OTHER INTERNATIONAL ORGANIZATIONS
- UNITED NATIONS AFFAIRS
- FINANCIAL MANAGEMENT

It was estimated that there would be 174 permanent positions in the Bureau of International Organization Affairs in fiscal 1967, as shown in Table II.[11]

TABLE II

	Estimated Number	Fiscal 1967 Estimate
Office of the Assistant Secretary	45	$542,021
Office of UN Political Affairs (UNP)	31	359,026
Office of Intl. Economic & Social Affairs (OES)	30	362,208
Office of Intl. Administration (OIA)	22	293,484
Office of Intl. Recruitment	9	101,451
Office of Intl. Conferences (OIC)	37	374,061
	174	$2,032,251

Source: United States. House of Representatives. Hearings before a Sub-committee of the Committee on Appropriations. *Departments of State, Justice, Commerce, etc. . . . for 1967.* 89th Congress, Second Session. 1966. p.239.

UNP and OES are substantive and the other offices are administrative, but these matters overlap on occasion so that no clear distinction can be maintained.

Office of United Nations Political Affairs (UNP). This office has three main responsibilities: (1) It discharges the "action responsibilities" — those which involve substantive decisions—of the Assistant Secretary on U.N. political and security matters and reviews such matters which arise in other international bodies. (2) It formu-

---

[11] The geographic bureaus in the Department of State are much larger than 10. In these bureaus, the numbers of permanent positions in 1965 were as follows: African Affairs—1274, Near Eastern and South Asian Affairs—1386, Far Eastern Affairs—1503, Inter-American Affairs—1520, and European Affairs—3734. (Hearings before a Subcommittee of the Committee on Appropriations, House of Representatives, 89th Congress, 1st session. *Departments of State... [etc.] for 1966 Washington,* 1965, p.18.

lates—with the advice, review, and concurrence of other appropriate agencies of the government—and transmits to United States representatives in UN bodies the policy of the Department of State on international security matters, including, for example, disarmament, the peaceful use of atomic energy, and the development of procedures and programs needed for UN enforcement measures in the maintenance or restoration of international peace by UN agencies. It also deals with the pacific settlement of international political disputes or situations which arise in the UN and the development of procedures necessary for making such settlements possible. (3) It coordinates and supervises the over-all preparations for sessions of the General Assembly.

The office is headed by a director and two deputies. Other members of the staff are assigned specific topics with which to deal: for example, in 1965 one staff member was responsible for the UN Charter and its constitutional history, charter review, membership, the enlargement of councils, and the organization of the UN Secretariat; another dealt with Article 19 and the loss of voting privileges, the political aspects of human rights and UN financing; and a third looked after Arab-Israel problems, UNRWA, Oman, Jordan waters, UNEF, Aden, and logistical assistance to UN operations in Cyprus and the Middle East.

The staff members in UNP are grouped under the headings listed in the organization chart: United Nations Political Affairs, Dependent Area Affairs, General Assembly and UN Organization Affairs, and International Security Affairs. Each has staff members who concentrate on specific matters within that area.

To illustrate the work of UNP, in the "missile crisis" in Cyprus in 1965, the UN was informed and it, in turn, notified member-governments. The USUN sent word to the Department of State in Washington where the Message Center distributed copies to all departmental officers who needed them. Meanwhile, American Embassy officials in Cyprus also reported to the department. The "action copy" of this telegram went to a department officer, either in UNP or perhaps a desk officer, and "information copies" to all others concerned. The officer receiving the "action copy" was responsible for formulating a position that, when approved, became the American government's policy on this matter.

No one man, of course, has the full responsibility for so critical a portion of the country's foreign policy. To obtain approval, the official with the "action copy" must consult with all other concerned officers in the department in order to arrive at a common agreement. In fact, those needing to be consulted at an early stage of the 1965 Cyprus "missile crisis" included the desk officers in the Office of Greek, Turkish, and Iranian Affairs in the Bureau of Near Eastern and South Asian Affairs. Such desk officers were also experts on Cyprus but they were concerned with this island as part of an area while the other man dealt with it as a problem for the UN. Since the news in March 1965 suggested that the missiles were being transported to Cyprus from Egypt, the Egyptian desk officer was also concerned as was the Soviet Union desk officer since the missiles presumably originated there.

The Office of Western European Affairs was also involved, because of its relation to NATO: the desk officer for Great Britain, because that country has a continuing interest in and responsibility for its former colony; the office of the State Department's Legal Adviser, if there were special legal problems; the office of Intelligence and Research might have information and opinion about the matter; the Office of the Assistant Secretary for Public Affairs needed to be informed because the landing of missiles on Cyprus would be headline news and its presentation to the press, radio and television would require coordination with the substantive decision of the Department; the Congressional Relations office probably wanted information, so that certain Congressmen could be notified in advance and Congressional opinion assessed; while the Bureau of Economic Affairs maintained an interest in munitions control, resources, and transportation.

The UNP officer may not be able to secure agreement readily from all of his colleagues and such a problem is usually raised to a higher level within the department. The Assistant Secretary may have to be notified of a failure of consensus at the lower level and need to con-sult other assistant secretaries or they may have to appeal to the Under-Secretary or the Secretary of State. However, few matters, probably less than 10%, need to rise above the level of assistant secretaries.

Information copies of all important telegrams go to all higher officers of the Department of State. The Secretary has an executive secretariat to bring to his attention those which he "needs to see." Some are condensed in the daily summary available to high-level officials in the department. Certain of these matters are discussed at the Secretary's morning staff conference, and the Policy Planning staff may also be asked to consider some.

At some point in all this consultation, however, the Department of State officials do reach agreement, but the department is not yet ready to send instructions to the United States Representative at the UN. To illustrate again, in the Cyprus question other departments or agencies or the government were also interested. Any matter of missiles, for example, was of concern to the Department of Defense. Interdepartmental agreement may be more difficult than intradepartmental agreement. In any case, a system of continuous consultation ["clearance" is the word used in the Department of State] among the federal agencies ensures that the United States policy presented in the UN will be indeed the policy of the American government.

There has been criticism of this clearance procedure. "The procedures of the U. S. Government for making policy decisions regarding issues before the United Nations," wrote Senator Aiken in 1961 after having seen this situation as a delegate to the General Assembly, "are exasperatingly slow and cumbersome. I strongly recommend to President Kennedy that he undertake to reconstruct the processes of our Government so that decisions can be made promptly and responsibility can be fixed for failure to make them."[12] And two years later, after they had been delegates to the General Assembly, Senators Gore and Allott wrote that "One stumbling block lies in trying to get . . . ideas through the bureaucratic machinery to the decision-making level."[13]

The clearance process can produce policy that represents the lowest common denominator of mutual agreement, so innocuous that, while it satisfies all of the many participants, it loses most of its dynamism. New ideas may be stifled as a premium is placed on the status quo, one of the earmarks of bureaucracy. Yet, important decisions on vital foreign policy matters should not be made by minor officials of the Department of State. Their function is not to change the direction of American foreign policy but to apply policies already adopted, and to find the best tactics for doing so. New ideas should be tempered in the fire of departmental discussion. As be-

---

[12] *The United States in the United Nations.* Supplementary report to the Committee on Foreign Relations by Senator George D. Aiken, U. S. Senate, 87th Cong., 1st Sess., February 1961, p.2.

[13] *The 18th General Assembly of the United Nations.* Report by Sen. Albert Gore and Sen. Gordon Allott to the Committee on Foreign Relations and Committee on Appropriations, U. S. Senate, 88th Cong., 1st Sess., February 1963, p.3.

tween the extremes of caution and boldness, the former may well be the better, especially in foreign relations. The department may have been unduly cautious in recent years, as some of its critics maintain, but it is not apparent that the criticism would have been less had the department plunged carelessly and boldly ahead into the danger of a nuclear world.

Almost all important political problems come before the UN at some stage and are then dumped in the lap of UNP in Washington. Because some of their problems are "hot and glamorous," threatening to escalate into crises rather rapidly, UNP officials try to maintain a substantial flexibility. At one period interdepartmental committees were used for face-to-face consultation and presumably for quick agreement. But it was found that much of the discussion did not center around "UN business" and often when an operational officer was detached from his other duties to attend these meetings, his time was wasted. A task force was created, to deal with the Berlin situation, for example, but UNP was only a "partial participant" and little by little it reduced its relation to the task force. UNP officers now prefer informal, direct contacts on an *ad hoc* basis.

By the nature of its work, this office normally has direct access to higher officials, including the Assistant Secretary, the Secretary, or even the White House. There are times, however, when minutes count in deciding policy and when the Department of State may have to recommend a decision to the President without much consultation with other parts of the government. When the first news of North Korean aggression reached Washington on 24 June 1950, for example, the President, the Secretary of State, and the Counselor of the State Department were all absent from the city. The first group that met to assess this development consisted of Philip C. Jessup (Ambassador-at-large), Dean Rusk (Assistant

Secretary of State for Far Eastern Affairs), John D. Hickerson (Assistant Secretary of State for United Nations Affairs), H. Freeman Matthews (Deputy Under-Secretary of State), and Frank Pace (Secretary of the Army). These men held important, relevant positions and understood the nature of this crisis. By the next day, the President, the Secretary of State, the Secretary of Defense, and the Joint Chiefs of Staff were present, informed and able to decide on policy. Throughout that week, the important decisions were made by informal groups and not by the regular institutional units; neither the National Security Council nor the permanent officials of the Department of State seem to have played an important role.

A similar process seems to have occurred during the Cuban missile crisis in October 1962. President Kennedy asked a group of about fifteen top-level officials to put aside all other duties so they could make an intensive survey of the situation and the alternatives for action. For these men the next week was filled with a continuing series of meetings. "No one outside that group knew a crisis was brewing;"[14] neither the Cabinet nor the National Security Council was called into session. Every precaution was taken to prevent anyone else from knowing what was going on, although James Reston reported that the President indicated to certain Cabinet members his intentions after policy had been set.[15] There was only one mention of officials below the Cabinet level: "Assistant secretaries differed vigorously with their secretaries."[16] Otherwise there was no reference to those outside this small group and no suggestion that any consultation occurred within the departments or between de-

---

[14] *New York Times*, October 23, 1962, p.19.

[15] *Ibid.*, October 26, 1962, p.30.

[16] Theodore C. Sorensen, "Kennedy vs. Khrushchev: The Showdown in Cuba," *Look*, vol. 29, September 7, 1965, p.46.

partmental staffs with "clearance" in the normal sense.[17]
The President dealt with that crisis in "the new Kennedy
style of diplomacy . . . power diplomacy in the old classic
European sense that prevailed before the great men
worried much about consulting with allies or parliaments
or international organizations."[18]

Once the basic decisions had been made, the processes of consultation were resumed, including consultation with the Latin American foreign ministers and sub-
mission of the problem to the UN Security Council.

In a crisis, then, UNP may play no role at all. But
there are thousands of other policy matters in which
UNP prepares the field and largely determines the decisions.

*Office of International Economic and Social Affairs
(OES)*. The second substantive part of the Bureau of
International Organization Affairs is the Office of International Economic and Social Affairs (OES), which discharges the substantive responsibilities of the Bureau
for American policies and programs pertaining to ECO-
SOC, its subsidiary bodies and the specialized agencies;
social, health, human rights and freedom of information
matters; and relationships with non-governmental organizations. The Office also aids in the coordination of
UN and United States technical assistance programs. If
the short-run success of the United Nations depends
largely on its success in the political and security field,
the long-run evaluation may rest upon the organization's
success in the fields of social and economic programs.

---

[17] Indeed, Schlesinger specifically states that during the consideration of the Bay of Pigs invasion, "The men at the State
Department's Cuban desk, who received the daily flow of
information from the island, were not asked to comment on
the feasibility of the venture," Arthur M. Schlesinger, Jr., "The
Bay of Pigs — 'A Horribly Expensive Lesson,' " *Life*, vol. 59.
July 23, 1965, p.67.

[18] James Reston, *New York Times*, October 26, 1962, p.30.

There are seven subdivisions in OES, each with officers responsible for specific aspects of the Office's work. There are problems of definition of responsibilities, for almost all the UN topics have political implications. Nevertheless, all items are not sent to UNP. One distinction comes from the spheres of the General Assembly's main committees. Basically, what goes to Committee I (Political) goes to UNP, what goes to Committees II (Economic and Financial), and III (Social, Humanitarian, and Cultural) goes to OES. Whom will the United States support for the post of Secretary General? Should the Republic of South Africa be expelled from a particular UN agency because of its apartheid policy? These are clearly political questions. Presumably the question of whether to expand a malaria control program is social and not political, although if an increased expenditure for malaria control in Greece means that there will be no program to control yaws in Haiti, the question may also be political. Such grey, fringe zones cause the problems.

In the early days of the UN, political considerations were the main element in deciding what candidates to support for certain offices in the organizations. But in the last years it has been recognized that this is not a clear political matter and that a knowledge of the personalities involved may be more important than which governments are represented. Since OES is more likely to know these individuals than UNP, the former group makes initial recommendations for agencies with which it deals, consulting UNP and the geographical bureaus. By general acceptance, anything which involves the question of Chinese representation in any UN body goes automatically to UNP, but both OES and UNP deal with questions of Portuguese or South African representation in UNESCO or ILO, consulting the geographic bureaus of the Department. One departmental officer said that only very rarely is there a jurisdictional problem between UNP and the OES.

By statutory provision, matters dealing with international monetary and financial matters are handled by the National Advisory Council, chaired by the Treasury Department. Normally whatever NAC suggests is the final policy although OES goes through the formality of clearing the position through IO since the Assistant Secretary has to sign the instruction.

By and large, the clearance process indicated earlier in UNP is followed in OES. For example, the agenda of twelve items and the background papers for the 1965 ECOSOC meeting was parcelled out among the appropriate staff members for study, action, and clearance, a complicated process due to the very large number of federal government agencies interested in economic and social matters.

On the other hand, economic and social matters are unlikely to escalate into crises. In fact, almost every item on the agenda of ECOSOC, its subsidiary bodies, and the specialized agencies has been on the agenda before. The past American position normally is a guideline to policy at the next session, as with most governments. Delegations start in where they left off at the last meeting. Circumstances sometimes change to create or revise policy: a new development on the international scene, a report from the last meeting that a certain stand was no longer helpful, or the initiative of the Assistant Secretary may impel OES to write a new position paper for approval by all interested agencies.

OES, unlike UNP, has often used interdepartmental committees for these clearance purposes. Four such committees have been: the Interdepartmental Committee on International Labor Policy, the Interdepartmental Committee on Narcotics, the Interdepartmental Committee on Foreign Policy relating to Human Rights, and the

United Nations Economic Committee. When general policy is approved by such a committee, OES writes the final position paper and also a clearance paper which summarizes the position and lists the agencies which have given approval if there has been disagreement. The clearance paper must point out all areas of disagreement, so that the Assistant Secretary will know the positions held by the various interested parties.

In some cases the substantive interest of another federal agency is great enough that it is given responsibility for developing positions on items in which OES is interested. This has frequently happened in the Interdepartmental Committee on International Labor Policy which is chaired by the Department of Labor. But OES has an officer who works on International Labor Organization matters almost exclusively and if he believes that the position advocated by the Department of Labor is inappropriate or indefensible, he can exercise a large degree of control over the policy.

One reason why it has been possible for UNP and OES to function effectively in the complex fields of their activity has been a high degree of continuity among the members of the staff of those offices.[19] The long memories of these officers, their knowledge of developments and precedents, and their familiarity with the individuals who deal with these topics provide important advantages to the American government. In 1965 the directors of OES and UNP were both Foreign Service officers, one of whom had been rotated to Washington less than a

---

[19] In 1965 there were in the Assistant Secretary's office, one man who had been there since 1945; in UNP one officer since 1941 and another since 1946 except for a three-year assignment overseas in 1960; in OES one since 1944, one since 1947, and a third since 1948. Joseph Sisco, who became Assistant Secretary-IO in the summer of 1965, was for many years a mainstay in UNP.

year before. Both relied heavily upon the experienced career officials in their offices for institutional memory.

This period of long experience may be ending. Under the Wristonization program,[20] it is not likely that in the future, anyone will have twenty years of uninterrupted service in the same type of work. There are both advantages and disadvantages to this system, but the past continuity has made it possible for the department to function in the first two decades of participation in international organizations as would otherwise not have been possible.[21]

Office of International Administration (OIA). The Office of International Administration (OIA) coordinates departmental policy on financial support for international organizations as well as the general administration and management of such organizations. This includes policy and proposals on personnel, financial, budgetary and other administrative matters of the United Nations and the specialized agencies, and the preparation of instructions and technical advice to American representatives in these organizations on such matters. It prepares the budget requests and justifications for the appropriations needed for American contributions to

---

[20] A special committee, headed by Henry Wriston, President of Brown University, recommended in 1954, among other things, that distinctions between the Foreign Service and the Department Service in Washington should be reduced by requiring officers to be rotated at intervals between service in Washington and service abroad. This practice—called "Wristonization"—has been widely adopted in the Department, so that long service in a single position is now much less likely than previously.

[21] In 1956, the beginnings of Wristonization came at the time of the almost simultaneous crises over Suez and Hungary. Many of the IO staff members were Foreign Service personnel who had just begun their "Washington service," and had not yet acquired great familiarity with the functioning of the Bureau or of the United Nations itself.

international organizations and programs, and administers the expenditure of these funds so far as the United States is concerned.

The organization of OIA is simpler than UNP and OES. The Director is aided by two deputy directors and two international administration officers who deal with passports and visas, privileges, immunities, and accreditations under the UN Headquarters Agreement, and administrative assistance to UN field missions. Most of the staff members in this office are assigned to the administrative relations with a specific group of international organizations. There is also a Budget and Financial Management Unit which is concerned with the management of American appropriations and the special financial problems involved in the United States position on contributions to international organizations.[22]

Office of International Conferences (OIC). The last office in IO to be discussed is OIC which makes the necessary organizational and administrative arrangements for participation by the American government in international conferences, determining the extent and character of participation and naming, but not selecting, the delegates. This work normally involves negotiations with other federal agencies. The office is also responsible for seeing that position papers are prepared by the proper agencies for these international meetings. When international conferences are held in the United States, OIC prepares and issues the invitations, programs, agenda, and rules of procedure.

The director of OIC serves as secretary for American delegations to conferences attended by the Secretary of State or other high officials of the government, and as

---

[22] The International Personnel Staff and the International Recruitment Service were part of OIA for several years but now constitute a separate unit, the Office of International Organization Recruitment.

Secretary-General for most major meetings in the United States. The Conference Program staff consists of ten program officers who supervise the coordination of the views of all interested government agencies as to the desirability and nature of American participation in any given conference, and the formation and instruction of the delegations. One of the program officers serves as Secretary of Delegation at an important conference. Each program officer is assigned certain organizations or topics, and is responsible for the preparations for all such conferences.

A second unit in OIC is Conference Administration to provide necessary administrative services and facilities. Its work is indicated by a checklist used in OIC by anyone responsible for a particular conference: position papers initiated and target date set by memorandum; liaison with the interested agencies; clearances recorded in OIC; covering instructions drafted; signatures; concurrences; short form instructions in lieu of position papers; delegation instructions and documents; and drafted full-powers request to Legal Office.

After each conference, moreover, the following items must be checked: summary statement of American participation; fiscal report; distribution request submitted; letters of appreciation from delegation chairmen prepared; official delegation reports received; distribution recommended; official delegation reports acknowledged; delegation report reviewed for new conferences and items for implementation; and analysis of the value of the conference to the United States, and attitude toward future conferences.

The administration of the conference itself provides the longest part of the checklist: information from Mission, passports, inoculations, transportation, excess baggage, secretarial personnel requested, hotel reservations, office arrangements, supplies and equipment, invitations engraved, joint room assignments, communications arrangements, communications code name, departure telegram, notification to families of arrival, delegation security arrangements, delegation meeting, customs courtesies for returning VIPs, return arrangements, administrative officer report, departure kits, travel orders, budget estimate, travel advance, delegation of authority letters, fiscal instructions, and legal problems. Many hours of long, tedious, but indispensable work are involved in organizing and holding conferences. A former Assistant Secretary of State of IO has said that this Conference Administration Staff doesn't do the delegation's laundry, but that it does just about everything else.

OIC is not responsible for the substantive matters involved in conference participation, but for the administrative problem of seeing that each bureau or office of the department, or in the government, prepares its substantive positions for incorporation in the approved instructions to delegates. OIC normally seeks to keep the delegations to conferences as small as possible while UNP or OES desire larger groups; one looks at the budget, the other at the presentation of views. While OIC is charged with naming the members of the delegation, the substance of the agenda generally determines the selection. OIC does not participate in the policy clearance process as OES does nor write clearance papers. OES, accordingly, would like to select delegation members for conferences in which it is interested. On most occasions, however, there seems to be little difficulty as to which individuals should be members of a delegation, for certain agencies must be represented and only a few individuals can be considered for the posts.

3

United Nations
Conferences and
the United States

Since 1945 America has been increasingly and deeply involved in multilateral diplomacy. In the nineteenth century, the United States participated in an average of one international conference a year; from 1901 to 1925, an average of seven a year; and from 1926 through the end of World War II, an average of forty-one a year. Then came the deluge. In fiscal 1961, for example, the American government sent delegations to 381 international conferences; in 1963 to 547; and in 1964 to 580. More than half of these meetings were within the framework of the United Nations system.

Budget requests for international conference costs in fiscal 1965 included $565,950 for the principal UN organs, $689,000 for the specialized agencies, and $1,168,-000 for other international organizations and conferences, making a total of $2,431,000. Some Congressmen have considered this an excessive amount, yet for five years, despite an increase of nearly sixty per cent in the number of conferences in which the United States has participated, the basic appropriation was frozen at $1,943,000.[23] Involved here, of course, is the serious problem of whether or not such a continuing financial restriction adversely affects the international interests of the United States. Although the State Department has repeatedly requested Congress to appropriate more money for international conferences, it apparently has not convinced Congress that the restriction impairs the influence of America in world affairs.

The President of the United States appoints official representatives to international conferences, but in practice this has been delegated to the Secretary of State and the Assistant Secretary-IO except where the law requires delegates to be designated by the President himself.

Congress now requires that the Senate confirm appointments to the United States delegations to most international organizations and conferences. Normally the Senate has not interfered with such presidential nominations, although in 1951 when Truman selected Philip Jessup as a delegate to the 6th General Assembly, Senator Joseph McCarthy and Harold Stassen attacked the appointment on the grounds that Jessup had "an affinity for Communism." There was a full hearing by a subcommittee of the Senate Foreign Relations Committee which, in the end, refused to approve this nomination even though only one member accepted the charges made against Jessup. Three days after Congress adjourned, Jessup was given a recess appointment by the

---

[23] Hearings before the subcommittee of the Committee on Appropriations, U. S. Senate, 88th Cong., 2nd Sess., Depts. of State. . . [etc.] for the fiscal year ending June 30, 1965, p.562.

President. Every member of an American delegation must have a security clearance before he can be officially accredited. Permanent government officials will already have been cleared. By law, delegates to WHO and ILO meetings, including members of Congress and those holding Presidential appointments, require a complete security investigation. For almost all meetings, delegates have an instruction and a position paper prepared by OIC and signed by the Assistant Secretary of State-IO. This theoretically safeguards the interests of the American government against delegates who might presume to speak their own views or commit the government without prior approval from Washington.

Composition of United States Delegations. United States delegations to international conferences may consist of mixtures of officials of the American government and public members (those who hold no official posts), so that in a single year two dozen government agencies and a hundred public groups in the country will be represented by those going to international conferences, some in the role of delegates and others as advisers. The delegations are often small, two or three delegates and an equal number of advisers. To a special conference such as that on the Law of the Sea in Geneva in 1958, the United States sent a half dozen delegates and a large group of advisers representing a dozen federal government agencies and an almost equal number of private groups interested in various aspects of marine activity.

The largest delegations are those sent to the annual sessions of the General Assembly. Under the Charter no government may send more than five representatives to the General Assembly, with the Rules of Procedure allowing five additional alternates and such advisers as may be required by the delegation. At the 19th General Assembly in 1964 the United States delegation consisted of 84 persons as follows:

	Representatives and Alternates	Advisers	Total
United States Mission to the UN	5	44	49
Department of State	2	28	30
United States Senate	2	1	3
Other	1	1	2
Total	10	74	84

The 30 members from the Department of State came from: IO-14; regional geographic bureaus-6; Legal Adviser's Office-4; Arms Control and Disarmament Agency-3; Foreign Service-2; Cultural Affairs-1.

Another aspect of the composition of the delegation, especially to the main councils of the United Nations, has been the issue of democratic representativeness versus professionalism. The United States in recent years has always made purely political appointments for regular ambassadors but the wisdom of that practice in multilateral diplomacy is still unclear.

The United States permanent representatives to the United Nations have been highly qualified in public service, but their backgrounds have been primarily in domestic politics rather than international diplomacy. In forming the rest of the delegations to the General Assembly, moreover, the Department of State has been moved more by the political representation of the delegates than by their professional diplomatic skill. "The U. S. Delegation to the General Assembly," wrote two delegates, "must be widely representative of the varied interests, backgrounds, and cultural as well as racial origins of the American people,"[24] and the government has quite consistently followed the practice of including

---

[24] *Report on the 14th Session of the General Assembly of the United Nations,* by Hon. Clement J. Zablocki and Hon. James G. Fulton of the Committee on Foreign Affairs, 86th Cong., 2d sess., Union Calendar No. 593, House Report No. 1385, March 14, 1960, p.3.

on the delegation two members of Congress, a Roman Catholic, a Jew, a Negro, a woman, and often a labor leader.[25]

Some have asserted that the presence of a Negro on the delegation is helpful to the American image at home and abroad. Dr. Zelma George, a Negro from Cleveland worked with many of the African delegates at the 1960 General Assembly, and the distinguished singer, Marian Anderson, was a member of the United States delegation in 1958. Both these women, however, publicly disagreed with the American position on African questions, contrary to the spirit of professional diplomats who may disagree with policy but submerge their personal feelings and maintain an appearance of unity within the delegation. Some have considered the appointment of a woman, regardless of color, politically desirable. Mrs. Eleanor Roosevelt wrote, "I knew that as the only woman on the delegation I was not very welcome. Moreover, if I failed to be a useful member, it would not be considered merely that I as an individual had failed, but that all women had failed and there would be little

---

[25] Thus in 1959, in addition to the two members of Congress just quoted, the delegation consisted of Henry Cabbot Lodge and James J. Wadsworth, the two chief United States representatives at the UN who were already experienced in UN affairs, George Meany, President of the American Federation of Labor-Congress of Industrial Organizations and Walter S. Robertson, an investment banker from Richmond and former Assistant Secretary of State for Far Eastern Affairs. The alternates were Charles W. Anderson, Jr., a lawyer, former member of the Kentucky legislature, and Assistant Commonwealth Attorney in Kentucky; Earle Cocke, Jr., business and civic leader in Georgia, vice president of Delta Air Lines, and former national commander of the American Legion; Virgil M. Hancher, president of the State University of Iowa; Mary P. (Mrs. Oswald) Lord, long active in UN affairs, including service at six General Assemblies; and Harold Riegelman, lawyer, former chairman of a special UN Committee on Tax Problems of UN Delegations, and member of the Administrative Tribunal of the UN.

chance for others to serve in the near future."[26] Near
the end of the 1st General Assembly, Senator Vandenberg and John Foster Dulles told her candidly that they
had begged the President not to nominate her, but
admitted in sincerity they had worked with her gladly,
and would be happy to do so again.[27] The non-profes-
sionals on the delegations have offered some problems,
but they have also rendered some very useful service.
Nevertheless, as the UN has developed power, as many
significant political problems have come to the UN for
settlement, as the technical problems of economic and
social development have played a more important role
in UN activities, the question continues to be raised as
to whether delegates skilled in manufacturing, music,
civic clubs, and labor organization can represent the
United States in multilateral diplomacy better than officials experienced in international affairs.

In recent years, a new emphasis on professionalism
has appeared in the American delegations to the UN.
In 1961 of the five delegates and five alternates to the
General Assembly almost all had had experience with the
State Department or the UN system. In 1964 the five
delegates to the 19th General Assembly were Adlai
Stevenson, William C. Foster, and Francis T. P. Plimp-
ton, each familiar with the UN system, and two members
of the Senate, while the alternates were Charles Yost,
Charles Noyes, and Gladys (Mrs. Charles) Tillett, each
with years of diplomatic and UN experience. In addition, Richard N. Gardner, was Deputy Assistant Secretary of State-IO, and Franklin H. Williams had served
with the Peace Corps as well as maintaining a special
interest in African affairs. Thus, the delegation consisted
almost entirely of trained diplomats with experience in

---

[26] Eleanor Roosevelt, *On My Own*, New York, Harper, 1958,
p.47.
   [27] *Ibid.*, p.53.

the United Nations, except for the two Senators whose presence was the one obeisance to domestic politics.

In 1965 the five delegates to the 20th General Assembly were Arthur Goldberg, Charles Yost, and William C. Foster, each familiar with the UN system, and two members of the House of Representatives. The alternates were James M. Nabrit, Jr., President of Howard University and newly-appointed Deputy United States Reppresentative to the Security Council, Eugenie M. (Mrs. John E.) Anderson and Miss Frances Willis, both with years of service as United States Ambassadors, James Roosevelt, former member of the House of Representatives, and William P. Rogers, former Attorney General of the United States. Seven of this group were experienced in UN affairs and diplomacy although three of this number were new appointees to their posts.

It is too soon to conclude that the old system has now been permanently abandoned, but there has been a noticeable change in the type of American representation at the UN with increasing experience and professionalism in world affairs. One weakness of United States delegations to the General Assembly has been that several members may be serving for the first time and are thus quite unfamiliar with the UN system. At least three or four of the ten members probably should have had previous UN experience to give the delegation maximum usefulness from the very beginning of the General Assembly sessions.

In sum, OIC has a key responsibility for the success of American diplomacy in the UN, for it must coordinate a dozen federal agencies, as they help to select delegation members and as UN position papers are prepared. But policy matters largely turn upon the work of the professional, full-time, year-round mission of the United States assigned to the UN.

4

The United States Mission to the United Nations: Corridor Diplomacy

In the case of bilateral diplomacy the United States maintains a diplomatic mission in the capital of the host country and the mission has a direct relation with one of the five geographic offices in the Department of State; for multilateral organizations, the United States has developed a series of comparable missions accredited to the organizations, in direct relationship with the Bureau of International Organization Affairs. For the UN, this is the United States Mission to the United Nations (USUN) which is the main channel between the Department of State and the various UN agencies as well as with missions sent to the UN by other governments. As Ambassador Henry C. Lodge once said, the UN has become "the greatest single diplomatic crossroads in the world."[28]

---

[28] Quoted in Chadwick F. Alger, *United States Representation in the United Nations,* Report prepared for the Carnegie Endowment for International Peace, New York, 1961, p.5.

USUN consists of those who are assigned full-time and "permanently" to the mission, but not members of the United States delegation to the General Assembly except as members of the mission may also be delegates.[29]

The United States maintains a number of other missions to deal with the work of UN agencies. The most important of these is the United States Mission to the European Office of the United Nations and other international organizations in Geneva, Switzerland. This mission has important relations with ECOSOC which holds frequent meetings in Geneva, and with the UN specialized agencies, ILO, ITU, WHO, and the World Meteorological Organization (WMO) , which have their headquarters and many of their meetings there. The mission is also involved with meetings of the UN Economic Commission for Europe (ECE) , refugee and migration work of the UN, conferences on arms control and disarmament, trade negotiations in connection with the General Agreement on Tariffs and Trade (GATT) , the European Free Trade Association (EFTA) and the UN Conference on Trade and Development (UNCTAD) . The Mission in Geneva is a busy place, since more than 100 international organizations have headquarters there, and in some years there are more, although smaller, international conferences in Geneva than at the UN in New York. The American government must keep in close touch with all these activities and in 1965 the staff of its mission in Geneva numbered 117.

The United States also maintains separate missions to the International Civil Aviation Organization (ICAO) in Montreal and to the International Atomic Energy Agency (IAEA) in Vienna. Where UN specialized agencies have

---

[29] Technically the delegation is part of the mission, under the Presidential designation, but there is a budgetary difference and representatives to the UN are given instructions as delegates and not as part of USUN.

headquarters elsewhere, such as FAO in Rome, the appropriate American Embassy takes charge of the liason work between the United States government and the agency. But most of American relations with the UN are handled at UN headquarters in New York through USUN.

Organization and Staff. USUN is headed by the Permanent United States Representative to the UN, two deputy permanent representatives, one representative to the Economic and Social Council and one to the Trusteeship Council, and the Counselor of the Mission. All now carry the rank of Ambassador except the Counselor who is a Minister. The remainder of the mission is divided into sections according to their functional activities, as shown in the following chart.

Contrary to normal bureaucratic growth, the mission was largest in the late 1940's and became smaller thereafter, with some increase in the last few years, as the following table of authorized personnel indicates.[30]

United States Mission to the UN—Number of Staff

1947—165	1951—195	1955—110
1948—212	1952—180	1960—108
1949—190	1953—155	1961—106
1950—196	1954—115	1962—134
		1965—126
		1966—110

---

[30] A study of the 78 permanent missions to the UN in 1960—Iceland, Libya, and Nepal used their embassies in Washington for this purpose except when the General Assembly was in session—showed that most of the missions were very small, as this table demonstrates:

No. Members of Mission	No. of Missions
1-3	14
4-6	31
7-9	20
10-15	8
16-24	2
25 or more	3

(Gary L. Best, "Diplomacy in the United Nations," unpublished dissertation, Northwestern University, August 1960, p.90.)

The Permanent Representative in 1965 appealed for more staff on the grounds of increased membership of the UN, the number and duration of meetings, and the growing number of agenda items. Counting diplomatic personnel only, the American mission was second in size with 44, to the Soviet mission which had 51.

The United States mission requires a staff with skills in parliamentary debate, conduct of negotiations, collection of political intelligence, familiarity with UN procedures, and an understanding of the problems in various parts of the world. Congressmen who have been members of United States delegations to the General Assembly have been favorably impressed by the effectiveness of the mission personnel.

There has been some question about the desirability of rotating mission staff to the Department of State and overseas posts, along lines now required for the Foreign Service generally. It is alleged that many Foreign Service officers are not sympathetic to the UN system and that more officers should become familiar with USUN and its work. Rotation thus could be helpful to the mission, to Washington and to other Foreign Service posts. Too long a service at the mission, however, could lead to a psychological distance between USUN and the Department, with men in New York "fighting the bureaucrats;" moreover, service at USUN has not been considered by many Foreign Service officers as attractive as service in a geographic bureau in the Department, on the theory that the latter service is most directly related to promotion. Four years, therefore, has been suggested as the most suitable duration of a tour of duty with USUN.

Work of USUN. Generally speaking, the work of the mission consists of: (1) representing the United States in meetings of UN councils, commissions, and specialized agencies; (2) stating the position of the United States

UNITED STATES MISSION

(JANUARY

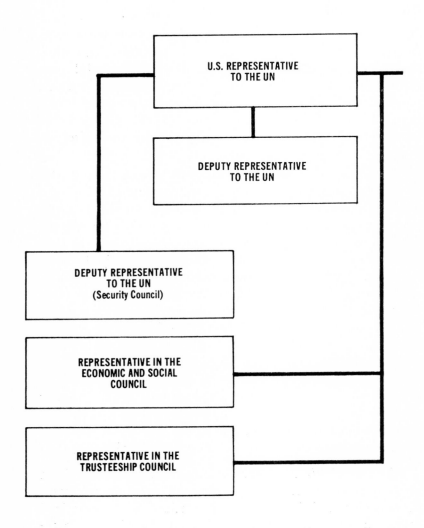

U.S. REPRESENTATIVE
TO THE UN

DEPUTY REPRESENTATIVE
TO THE UN

DEPUTY REPRESENTATIVE
TO THE UN
(Security Council)

REPRESENTATIVE IN THE
ECONOMIC AND SOCIAL
COUNCIL

REPRESENTATIVE IN THE
TRUSTEESHIP COUNCIL

TO THE UNITED NATIONS

1967)

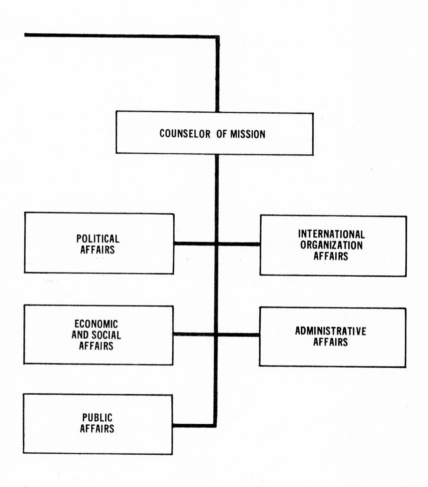

COUNSELOR OF MISSION

POLITICAL
AFFAIRS

INTERNATIONAL
ORGANIZATION
AFFAIRS

ECONOMIC
AND SOCIAL
AFFAIRS

ADMINISTRATIVE
AFFAIRS

PUBLIC
AFFAIRS

government on all issues under debate and the justifica-
tion of that position; (3) consulting and negotiating with
other delegations at the UN in an effort to obtain approval of American policies; (4) reporting to Washington on these activities; (5) advising the United States
government; and (6) maintaining contact with the Secretariat of the UN and other staffs of UN bodies.

As the organization chart of USUN shows, the mission
is further divided into five main sections; Administrative,
Public Affairs, International Organization Affairs, Political Affairs, and Economic and Social Affairs.

The Administrative Affairs Section contains personnel,
budget and fiscal officers, protocol officers, travel clerks,
and others to handle the general administrative work of
the Mission and of delegates to UN meetings.

The Public Affairs Section keeps mission officers informed on public opinion at home and abroad, on issues
before the UN, and it provides world news media with
press releases and background information essential to
an understanding of these issues. With 800 newsmen and
900 radio, television, and newsreel men accredited to the
General Assembly—of whom 40 to 50 are present daily—
the UN has become, in many ways, a more important
news-gathering center than Washington, and the American government is conscious of the need to provide an
understanding of American positions if its views are to
be understood overseas. The United States Information
Agency has at least one representative on the USUN
staff at all times, to make news and interpretations available through our overseas mission. The mission   staff
includes six information and public affairs specialists.

The International Organization Affairs Section deals
with the UN Secretariat on questions arising from the
1947 Headquarters Agreement and the fact that 5,000

members of this diplomatic community live in the United States. The United States has "host country" responsibilities, including customs, immigration, visa, identification, and diplomatic privileges and immunities problems for members of foreign missions to the UN, foreign delegates to UN meetings, and the UN Secretariat.[31] The section also works with legal matters being discussed in Committee VI, including budgetary and administrative matters which have legal aspects.

The Political Affairs and the Economic and Social Affairs sections deal with the substantive problems which arise in the UN. Their work of liaison, consultation, and negotiation with foreign diplomats will be discussed later under the heading "Corridor Diplomacy."

Budget. The Fiscal 1966 budget for USUN was $1,512,000 of which $1,313,500 went for salaries and benefits. All other items were small. Officials of the mission and the Department of State have brought great pressure on Congress in recent years to provide financial support for the expenses of mission personnel. The government now provides the Permanent Representative with a $30,000 suite at the Waldorf Towers, a nine-room suite including a dining room which seats about 50. For years $17,000 was allotted for representation allowances but this has recently been increased to $30,000. In 1963 the Permanent Representative attempted to secure housing allowances for certain mission personnel, pointing out that informal, home-like entertainment was an essential part of the work of some twenty officers in the mission but that few of them had sufficient personal wealth to buy or rent property close to the UN. American law

---

[31] Since 1962 the City of New York has also maintained an unsalaried Commissioner to the UN, to coordinate municipal services available to UN officials and delegates and improve relations between the government of the city and the UN.

gives housing allowances only to those stationed outside
the United States and Congress has thus far refused to
change it.

*The United States Permanent Representative to the
United Nations.* The mission in New York is headed by
the Permanent United States Representative to the UN.
His position as leader of the mission and as chief spokes-
man for the United States in UN councils has been clear.
His position in the American government has been less
so. All the United States representatives, Edward R.
Stettinius (1945-46), Warren R. Austin (1946-53),
Henry Cabot Lodge (1953-60), James J. Wadsworth
(1960-61), Adlai E. Stevenson (1961-65), and Arthur
Goldberg (1965-   ), have held the rank of Ambassador,
indicating the importance which the government attaches
to their work at the UN, for an ambassador has the
right of direct access to the President. Henry Cabot
Lodge was also made a member of the President's Cabinet
and later Wadsworth, Stevenson, and Goldberg were
similarly designated. There is a clear reason for placing
the United States Permanent Representative shoulder to
shoulder with the Secretary of State in the Cabinet, but
this complicates the position of the Assistant Secretary
of State-IO, who is not included in the Cabinet, although
he has charge of American policy in the UN.

Ambassador Austin was a quiet, peaceful man who
disliked public controversy. He caused no difficulty in
this hierarchical jumble. Lodge was much more dynamic
and assertive. At one time during the debate on the
Korean problem, he voted contrary to his instructions.
The Assistant Secretary of State, Robert Murphy, called
him on the telephone.

> "Apparently our instructions failed to reach you." Lodge
> repeated: "Instructions? I am not bound by instructions
> from the State Department. I am a member of the Presi-

dent's Cabinet and accept instructions only from him." I knew that personal and official relations between Lodge and the President were exceptionally close . . . But no one had warned me that Lodge regarded himself as independent of the State Department and I protested, "But you are also head of an embassy, and our ambassadors accept instructions from the Secretary of State." After a moment's pause, Lodge replied, "I will take note of the Department's opinions." . . . "This is a new situation to me," I said, "and I'll have to discuss it with the Secretary." Lodge replied coolly, "Yes, do that. He will set you straight." When I did report to Dulles, he listened carefully without comment until I finished, and then said, "This is one of those awkward situations which require special consideration. If it happens again, just tell me and I'll take care of it." . . . Once I understood that the Secretary of State did not choose to challenge the virtual autonomy which Lodge claimed for his embassy at the UN, I realized it was not appropriate for me to do so.[32]

In practice, however, this did not prove to be an impossible situation. Murphy admits that Lodge did accept ideas from the President and the Secretary "in good grace" and normally followed instructions from the Department. A former Assistant Secretary of State-IO agrees that Lodge came to see the desirability—indeed the necessity—of working with others and of cooperating with the government in Washington and quotes Lodge as saying, "I'm a good soldier. Tell me what you want me to do and I'll do it." Lodge had a mind of his own, with definite ideas which he set forth freely. Many believe that a good Ambassador should. "I thought he represented us very well indeed in New York."

When Adlai Stevenson was nominated to the UN by President John F. Kennedy, it was recalled that Kennedy once said that any Democratic President should offer

[32] Robert Murphy, *Diplomat Among Warriors,* New York, Doubleday and Co., 1964, p.367.

Stevenson the job of Secretary of State. What would Stevenson's relations be with Rusk and the President?, inquired Senator Hickenlooper during hearings before the Senate Foreign Relations Committee.

Sen. Hickenlooper: Do you have an understanding . . . that on matters that may come up . . . you will have the right to exercise your independent judgment without securing the guidance and approval of the State Department or the President?

Mr. Stevenson: I would hope that I could always have the guidance of the Secretary and the President, where necessary, in matters of that kind and that I should not be called upon to exercise independent judgment . . . without suitable consultation.

Sen. Hickenlooper: Do you anticipate that you will be given . . . a comparatively free hand, to determine American policy within the United Nations and, in effect, to have a veto in any way upon contrary positions taken by the Secretary of State.

Mr. Stevenson: No, I do not sir. I would not assert any such privilege. . . .

Sen. Hickenlooper: Therefore, in your position as Ambassador to the United Nations, I take it that your concept is that you will . . . be answerable principally to the President . . . and that the guidance followed by you will be that as laid down by the President or through the Secretary of State as the President's agent on international matters?

Mr. Stevenson: That is correct, Senator. I think the only difference which perhaps might not be clear . . . is that, to the extent that my time and circumstances permit, I would participate in the formation of policies that I would be called upon to execute.[33]

Both Lodge and Stevenson had access to the President. Frequently Stevenson spent one day a week in the

---

[33] Hearings before the Committee on Foreign Relations, U. S. Senate, 87th Cong., 1st Sess., on the proposed nomination of Adlai E. Stevenson as U. S. Representative to the UN, January 18, 1961, pp.14-16.

capital; he attended cabinet meetings regularly, some National Security Council meetings, and had frequent consultation with State Department officials. No evidence indicates that Stevenson appealed to the President to reverse decisions already taken in the Department and relations between him, the Secretary of State, and the Assistant Secretary of State-IO seemed to be entirely friendly and collaborative. The Ambassador went through regular channels to the Assistant Secretary as other Ambassadors do, and there was no appearance of a second foreign office in New York.

No previous American representative to the UN had such stature as Stevenson when he assumed this post. He had been present at the San Francisco conference as an advisor to the United States delegation, chief of the United States delegation to the Preparatory Commission in London, member of the United States delegation to the General Assembly in 1946 and 1947, and member of the committee which chose New York as the site for the UN. Stevenson was apparently given unusually great freedom in choosing an outstanding group of associates, some old friends and other professional diplomats.

This smoothly-functioning team was broken up in July 1965 by the sudden death of Adlai Stevenson when the issue of the obligation of certain members to pay their financial assessments for peace-keeping operations was still unresolved. President Lyndon Johnson lost little time in selecting a successor, Justice Arthur J. Goldberg of the Supreme Court, formerly Secretary of Labor. Although Goldberg had long been interested in foreign affairs, had traveled abroad, had represented President Kennedy on occasional foreign missions, and had been involved with ILO while Secretary of Labor, he had no experience in the multilateral diplomacy of the UN. He was, however, a trusted adviser to President Johnson and the President indicated by the appointment the high place that the United States government attributed to the UN post.

The *New York Times,* nevertheless, reported that the selection of Goldberg "caused great surprise and some dismay today when it became known. . . . To delegates of most foreign missions, the new Head of the U. S. Mission was merely a name that many of them said was completely unknown in their countries."[34] Others feared that because Goldberg was Jewish he might find it hard to deal impartially with questions involving Israel and her Arab neighbors. The United States government was sensitive enough about this matter to take unusual steps to make sure that he would not be initially handicapped at the UN, by arranging private meetings between the Assistant Secretary of State for African Affairs and diplomats from Morocco, Algeria, Tunisia, Libya, Kenya, the Sudan, Somalia, and Mauritania, while the Secretary of State invited the Tunisian and Moroccan ambassadors to the Department of State for additional talks. Most Arab delegates at the UN were noncommital on the selection, though one emphasized that the new American Ambassador would be supporting the policies of his government as made in Washington and not expressing his own personal views; and Goldberg himself tried to be reassuring. Appearing before the Senate Foreign Relations Committee at the hearing on his nomination, he said, "I shall be guided by the doctrine that in this pluralistic world, containing people of different religious beliefs and nations of differing political systems, all nations are to be treated with dignity, respect, fairness and equality. This is the policy of the United States . . . and that is my own personal faith."[35]

---

[34] *New York Times,* July 21, 1965, p.1.

[35] *Ibid.,* July 24, 1965, p. 6, The Committee quickly approved the nomination and, less than two hours later, the full Senate without debate voted unanimously to confirm him.

A month later, on August 25, President Johnson announced the selection of four aides to help Ambassador Goldberg. Of the previous group, only Charles Yost was retained, and he was promoted to become deputy to the Ambassador. James Nabrit, Jr., president of Howard University, became representative to the Security Council and, in the third ranking position, held the highest place ever given to a Negro at the mission. James Roosevelt, son of President Franklin D. Roosevelt and a member of the House of Representatives since 1954, was chosen as representative to ECOSOC and Eugenia (Mrs. John) Anderson, former ambassador to Denmark and minister to Bulgaria, became the representative to the Trusteeship Council. This team, except for Yost, had little experience in UN affairs, but presented a political, racial, and sexual balance in appointments. They were suggested to the President by the new Ambassador, after consultation with Secretary of State Rusk, and allowed Goldberg to have "his own group" to aid him in his new assignment. The replacement of the "Stevenson team" was complete when Yost resigned from USUN in April 1966 and Nabrit replaced him as Goldberg's deputy.

In the first few months at his new post, Ambassador Goldberg established an impressive record. Only a month after his arrival at USUN, he found himself, by the system of monthly alphabetical rotation, occupying the position of President of the Security Council, and was immediately confronted by the fighting between India and Pakistan, which he handled adroitly.

He also led the way in reversing the United States government position on the matter of penalizing the Soviet Union, France, and other countries by loss of vote in the General Assembly because of their failure to pay their peace-keeping assessments to the UN. Soon after he took office, moreover, Goldberg asked to meet with all the African Ambassadors at the UN and convinced them that he was not a personal threat to their position.[36]

One correspondent at the UN has written that "No American U. N. delegate has had such close ties with the White House as those enjoyed by Goldberg,"[37] while another stated that "Stevenson . . . was merely the representative of the United States; Ambassador Goldberg is the representative of Lyndon Johnson."[38] Goldberg and the President have consulted each other repeatedly during crises, on some occasions several times by telephone during a single night; Goldberg maintains an office in Washington and regularly attends Cabinet meetings. Many people feel that through Goldberg they have direct access to the White House.

Relations between the United States Permanent Representative to the UN, the Secretary of State, and the Assistant Secretary of State-IO have presented few problems in 1965 and 1966 and Goldberg, by inviting each Assistant Secretary in the Department of State to New York to meet UN representatives from the area of his special interest, and other devices, has become part of the State Department team.

For Goldberg, as for his predecessors, the work-load at USUN is backbreaking. Adlai Stevenson once said that "At the United Nations, I sometimes yearn for the peace and tranquility of a political campaign,"[39] and added that in four years he had had a total of eleven days of vaca-

---

[36] Of no small significance was an invitation to dinner later extended to Goldberg by the Ambassador of the United Arab Republic.

[37] Max Harrelson in *Syracuse Herald American*, November 24, 1965, p.11.

[38] Martin Mayer, "Goldberg Represents Lyndon Johnson," *New York Times Magazine*, February 6, 1966, p.16,

[39] *The New Yorker*, July 24, 1965, p.18. The following account of Stevenson's schedule is taken from pp.21-22 of this same article.

tion. In a "fairly routine" day early in 1965, for example, Stevenson spoke in the morning in the General Assembly in tribute to Winston Churchill who had just died, later conferred with members of his mission, after which he met with Secretary-General U Thant, then attended a luncheon given by the Chinese Ambassador to the UN, next meeting a group of American Congressmen, then conferring with the Norwegian Ambassador to the UN about a compromise plan to end the UN financial crisis, after which the new Ambassador from Malta to the UN paid him a courtesy call. After receiving eight other callers in the same afternoon, Stevenson went to a cocktail reception given by the American-Arab Association, then to a party launching an Indian exhibit, and finally returned to his apartment to change into formal clothes for a benefit ball for the Institute of International Education. At eight o'clock the next morning he was on a plane to Washington where he gave the memorial address for Churchill at the National Cathedral service and began an equally "routine" day.

Corridor Diplomacy. All missions at the UN try to win support for their policies and interests by adroit and careful backstage, personal negotiation often known as "corridor diplomacy." In the first years of the UN, the United States had an "automatic majority" in the General Assembly and generally speaking the major decisions of the General Assembly have not contradicted American security interests. With the large influx of new Asian and African states, the voting majority favorable to United States policies has become less certain, but many proposals presented by the American government represent to a considerable degree, positions suggested and agreed to, after mutual concessions, by a number of friends of the United States. As Secretary-General Hammarskjöld once said, "It is diplomacy, not speeches and votes, that continues to have the last word in the process of peace-making."[40] A necessary device in this kind of diplomacy is to ascertain the exact situation on an issue, to "take soundings." Action in the United Nations is not based on surprise, but on careful preparation. Public debate without such preparation is likely to be unproductive and may even be dangerous. The political advisers of the mission collect all possible information regarding the attitude of other delegations. In the process, it is possible for these advisers to make the American position known to the other delegations. At this kind of work, the American advisers have been called, "extremely persuasive and effective."[41] One scholar has noted that the United States "will try scrupulously to avoid stating a position on a question of any magnitude without first reaching an understanding with the United Kingdom."[42] To reach an understanding with all delegations would be impossible, but certainly when advance consultation has been inadequate any broad-based agreement in the General Assembly is doomed. Delegations have sometimes complained that the United States has acted without consulting them in advance. There are times when the United States prefers not to provide notice of its position, but normally such omissions result from the limitations of time and personnel available. An interesting example of this occurred in 1953 when the United States raised the question of atrocities committed against UN prisoners in Korea. Many delegates were surprised, for there had

---

[40] Dag Hammarskjöld, "The Element of Privacy in Peace-Making," *United Nations Review,* Vol. 4, # 9, March 1958, p.11.

[41] *6th Session of the General Assembly of the United Nations.* Report of the Committee on Foreign Affairs containing the report of Hon. Mike Mansfield and Hon. John M. Vorys, 82nd Cong., 2d Sess., Union Calendar No. 456, House Report No. 453, 1952, p.15.

[42] Robert E. Riggs, *Politics in the United Nations,* Urbana, Univ. of Illinois Press, 1958, p.33.

been no advance warning or consultation. This situation arose out of a lack of coordination between the Defense and State departments in Washington, for a report of such atrocities had been released by the Defense Department to appear in the newspapers on the morning of October 29, and before noon many Congressmen demanded that the United States take immediate action on the situation in the General Assembly. When Ambassador Lodge asked the Department of State for permission to place the item on the Assembly's agenda that day, there was no time for multilateral consultation.[43] In 1966, the American government suddenly decided over a weekend to take the Viet Nam situation to the UN, allowing the merest time for telephone calls and little consultation with other delegations.

Usually, however, the political schedule either permits or requires widespread advance consultation. For example, at the request of Ambassador Lodge, the American Atoms-For-Peace plan was outlined at a caucus of Latin American members of the UN, and comments and criticism invited, before the plan was presented to the 9th General Assembly in 1954. Secretary of State Dulles also appeared before the Latin American caucus that year to explain American policies in the Far East. Informal discussions of this type are likely to be more important than anything said later in the public debate and often the public debate becomes a formal ratification of understandings reached in the behind-the-scenes discussions.

Thus, members of the United States mission, especially the advisers and liaison officers, spend a great deal of time each day throughout the year talking with the delegates from other countries in the corridors or small committee rooms, over lunch or a drink, and at informal confer-

---

[43] Reported by Thomas J. Hamilton in the *New York Times*, November 6, 1953, p.6.

ences with small groups. A study in 1960 revealed that
86% of the representatives believed they had more contact with other diplomats when stationed at the UN than
when stationed in a national capital, even between sessions of the General Assembly, and 82% claimed that
such relations with diplomats were more informal at the
UN than in a national capital.[44] One delegate, indeed,
maintained that "the UN is our best overall observation
post. This is the best place to find out how the general
international winds are blowing,"[45] and Secretary-General Hammarskjöld stated in his 1959 Annual Report
that "the growing diplomatic contribution of the permanent delegations outside the public meetings . . . may
well come to be regarded as the most important 'common
law' development which has taken place so far within
the framework of the Charter."[46]

Certain American representatives have been particularly effective at this type of work. "Ernest Gross was
regarded as at his best in behind-the-scenes negotiations"
while James J. Wadsworth "made such a reputation in
quiet negotiations, negotiations in which he could keep
close personal friendship with diplomats whose policies
he strongly opposed,"[47] that the State Department twice
detached him from the mission in New York and sent
him to Europe where he could use this talent on other
important negotiations. One of the more publicized occasions in which corridor diplomacy aided American
purposes came in 1949. Carefully planned conversations
between Ambassador-at-large Philip C. Jessup and the

[44] Best, *op. cit.*, pp.121, 134.

[45] *Ibid.*, p.188.

[46] Dag Hammarskjöld, *Introduction to the Annual Report of the Secretary-General*, (Supplement # 1A), New York, 1959, p.2.

[47] John McVane, *Embassy Extraordinary: The U.S. Mission to the United Nations*, Public Affairs Pamphlet # 311, Public Affairs Committee, 1961, p.8.

Soviet representative, Jacob Malik, in the delegates' lounge at the UN, eventually led to an agreement that brought an end to the very dangerous blockade of Berlin.

Many of the smaller states do not give specific instructions to their UN delegation except on matters of direct concern to them or the delegates are uninformed about the American position. Whatever can be done by USUN to set its views before such delegates makes it that much more probable that the final instructions from their governments and their votes will satisfy the American government. Some of the delegates who are least informed are also the most sensitive to pressures from the Great Powers. Corridor diplomacy requires the most astute aspects of personal diplomacy, including familiarity with the culture and aspirations of such sensitive governments. The Department of State has often brought its area experts from abroad to New York, especially during General Assembly sessions, and sent desk officers from the Department to the UN at the same time. The United States delegation to the 19th General Assembly in 1964-65, for example, included representatives from the Department's Bureaus of African, Far Eastern, European, Inter-American, and Near Eastern and South Asian Affairs, as well as a large number of Department experts on political and security affairs and economic and social matters. In particular the American government included in the delegation Olcott H. Deming, its Ambassador to Uganda, who was brought home for the duration of the 19th General Assembly, because of the potential importance of African views and votes on matters coming before that session, and because of his experience with UN problems.

The normal session of a General Assembly confronts seventy to eighty substantive items. On each item, several alternative resolutions are often introduced. Each is likely to contain several parts, with dozens of key words inviting diplomatic negotiation. It may be important whether the General Assembly "notes" or "reaffirms" a previous resolution, whether it "calls upon" the parties to adjust differences or "expresses the hope" that they will do so, and so on. Opportunities for corridor diplomacy are practically endless in such matters and delicate negotiations unending.

This type of negotiation must be undertaken also in the selection of officers of UN bodies, such as the President of the General Assembly. Since the unwritten rule is that these offices are not held by delegates of the Great Powers, the competition among the smaller powers is often very keen. Governments frequently seek the support of the Department of State in an election which will not occur for a year or more. The same thing is true of the election of the non-permanent members of the Security Council, the members of ECOSOC, the Trusteeship Council, and the International Court of Justice. In all of these matters, careful planning is necessary to minimize or eliminate competition which will result in bad feelings among the free nations. The United States, as the leader of this group, is inevitably involved in this competition and must either participate in these election campaigns or accept whatever results ensue. In December, 1955, for example, the United States hoped to prevent the election of a Communist successor to Turkey on the Security Council but the coalition on which it depended collapsed. Although the American government might have been able to prevent the election of Yugoslavia, it would have had to pay an exorbitant price for such a victory. The defeat seemed doubly costly, not only because Yugoslavia was elected to the Council, but because members of the United Nations discovered how safely they could, on occasion, bolt American leadership.

Another device of corridor diplomacy is "arm twisting," the use of pressure to secure the desired support.

Here the political officers of USUN are particularly useful. A former adviser to the American delegation has described this process of "turning on the heat," as follows:[48]

> You sit down with the delegate, tell him the United States position, and ask for his support. . . . You . . . make his life miserable. Then he may say, "I'm cabling my government for instructions." You think he's lying so you cable his government; then you go to him with the cable. You keep after him until he gives in. No actual threats are made— it's just a process of hounding him to death.

The American liaison officer can do little but argue the merits of his government's position but his very insistence constitutes pressure. References to arm-twisting in the Department of State are usually jocular, but the serious aspect is frankly recognized. One technique is to ask the delegate to put his government's policy on the issue currently being discussed in the larger context of the relations between his country and the United States. On occasion, when the delegate is reluctant or when the American government wishes to reverse instructions already sent to him, American officials have applied pressure directly on the foreign office of the other country.

Reverse pressure, however, can be sometimes brought by other foreign offices upon the American government. At least once a year some government informs American officials that the position of the United States on a specific matter may well cause the other government to collapse or at least be rendered very unstable, so that officials in Washington must then decide how far to go in altering their already-determined position.

American pressure could result in virtual blackmail in cases where the distribution of economic aid is involved, although this is generally denied. As Ambassador Henry Cabot Lodge, Jr., told a House Committee

---

[48] Quoted in Riggs, *op. cit.,* p.37.

in 1953, "If we say they had better do what we tell them because we have got all the money, then that would irritate them. The worst thing we could do would be to do that."[49]

There are times when the United States prefers not to exert pressure on other delegations but is forced into such action by circumstances. An excellent example of this occurred in November 1947 during the General Assembly debate on the partition of Palestine. In the first stages of the debate the United States delegation merely confined itself to arguing the merits of partition, hoping that a sufficient number of delegations would support this idea so that it would not be necessary for the American government to bring any pressure on them and further antagonize the Arab governments. Nor did the American government wish to become so strong an advocate of partition that it would become responsible later for the implementation of the plan, especially since there were strong disagreements over the plan in the mission and in the Department of State itself. During the week of November 22, however, the attitude of the American government changed, for it was now feared that, without pressure, the partition plan would be defeated in the Assembly, with results which none could foresee. President Truman himself gave instructions to intervene strongly on behalf of the plan.

At other times the United States has been so vitally interested in achieving a goal in the UN that it brings all of its pressure to bear on members of that organization. In 1951 the United States wished the UN to declare the People's Republic of China an aggressor in Korea. American diplomats were reportedly[50] instructed

---

[49] House of Representatives, Subcommittee on Foreign Affairs, *Hearings on International Organizations and Movements,* March 27—July 29, 1953, 83rd Cong., 1st Sess., p.103.

[50] Riggs, *op. cit.,* pp.76-80, on which this account is based.

to tell the governments to which they were accredited that American public opinion might shift sharply if the UN ignored the Chinese aggression and that the fate of the UN might hinge upon the action taken by the General Assembly. On 18 January 1951 Ambassador Austin spoke on the issue in the General Assembly; on the same day President Harry Truman, in a press conference, stated that the United States would do everything it could to secure a condemnation of China. On January 19, the House of Representatives in an almost unanimous vote, approved a resolution that "the United Nations should immediately act and declare the Chinese Communist authorities an aggressor," and on January 23 the Senate unanimously requested the United Nations to reject the Chinese demand for membership and denounce that government as an aggressor. A week later, the General Assembly denounced China as an aggressor by a vote of 44-7-9. American pressure as well as evidence of Chinese aggression overcame the lack of enthusiasm for the resolution entertained by many members of the UN.

Normally the United States does not resort to such concerted action, for the success of corridor diplomacy depends very largely on the maintenance of a friendly atmosphere among the delegates to the United Nations.

One American Foreign Service Officer at USUN has observed that he thought of the delegates' lounge at the UN as "home," where over a period of months he found friends from all over the world as they came to UN meetings. It is an international clubhouse where almost every important government official is likely to be seen. As Ambassador Stevenson once said to the Senate Foreign Relations Committee, "To have on our shores, within the framework of free political institutions in the atmosphere of freedom, such an aggregation of political leadership provides an unparalleled opportunity to communicate the policies, the goals, and aspirations of the American people."[51]

Instructions from the Department of State. Another vital problem in USUN operations involves the instructions which come to New York from the Department of State in the form of telegrams, memoranda, or verbal telephone messages.

The United States mission, like any other diplomatic mission, regularly takes its instructions from the Department despite Ambassador Lodge's earlier views. Washington and USUN must be meshed together with the proper synchronization so that the American government may have one policy and one voice. Article 3 of the United Nations Participation Act provides that the representatives of the United States in the UN "shall, at all times, act in accordance with the instructions of the President transmitted by the Secretary of State unless other means of transmission is directed by the President and such representative shall, in accordance with such instructions cast any and all votes. . ." But does this mean that members of the mission sit and wait for instructions and then, like automatons, say the words and cast the votes as they have been told? The procedure is neither that mechanical nor that simple.

Members of the mission in New York take an active not a passive part in the formulation of policy for presentation in the UN. Being on the scene, knowing the current situation, being familiar with the diplomats present, members of USUN have information and judgment which no one in Washington can possess. A government which refused to consider this expertise and sensitivity would deny one of its best resources. On the political level, moreover, no Secretary of State is likely to

----

[51] Quoted in *You and the United Nations,* Department of State Publication 7442, December 1962, pp.4-5.

ignore the views of two important members of the House Foreign Affairs or the Senate Foreign Relations Committee in a delegation especially when they represent both political parties.

It is difficult for an outsider to judge just where initiative and decision lie in this delicately-poised relationship between Washington and New York. The fact seems to be that several officials are so interrelated in their work and in such close and constant contact that no one is "chief."

As indicated earlier, the Department of State, in coordination with other interested and related parts of the executive branch of American government, prepares the positions which fix policy on every UN agenda item. These positions may be broad or narrow, clear or vague. Mrs. Roosevelt wrote that Secretary of State George Marshall once gave her a State Department paper covering a subject under discussion.

> I read it carefully. Then I read it twice. Still I didn't know what our position was. I sent the paper around to one of the Department's best legal minds, and asked him to explain it to me. He sent me a note in reply: "If this is what they send to the President . . . God help the President!" Then I asked one of the delegation's most experienced advisers to come to my room. . . .
>
> "You must be able to explain this," I said. "You must have had a part in writing this paper."
>
> He studied it for a while and then said: "Yes, I had, but obviously it was not intended for you or anybody else to know what this paper meant."[52]

In any case, the fact that instructions have been signed by the Secretary of State and that the Assistant Secretary of State-IO is the chief focal point for coordination does not mean that the Department of State alone has de-

---

[52] Roosevelt, *op. cit.*, p.41.

cided the policy. USUN officials consult with other interested departments of the government and all can make comments, criticisms, or suggestions.

Normally as UN debate proceeds on the agenda items some revision of the national position is necessary, although the United States seems to have achieved a reputation for inflexibility on this point. A number of UN delegates told one interviewer that instructions were particularly rigid for both the Soviet and American delegations, and one Latin American delegate said, "The American delegation is in the least flexible position of any other delegation at the UN."[53] Of the delegations interviewed, two-thirds of them claimed to have the same amount of discretion in instructions at the UN as when stationed in a diplomatic mission at a foreign capital, and only six percent of them claimed to have less discretion at the UN, perhaps because the political situation changes so rapidly during a session of the General Assembly.[54]

The revision of positions is a continuing process. American delegates are in constant consultation with their advisers from the mission and the State Department as they deal with matters arising in their respective commissions or committees, and at least twice a week during sessions of the General Assembly there are full delegation conferences in the USUN building where the views of the delegates are coordinated before they leave for the sessions across the street at the UN. Frequently the conference has appealed to Washington for a change in instructions; in many cases there has been a modification. In the spring of 1949, for example, the American delegation strongly protested the decision of the Department of State to support the Latin American resolu-

[53] Best, *op. cit.*, p.162.
[54] *Ibid.*, pp.159, 161.

tion to lift the diplomatic embargo on Franco Spain and the delegation was later instructed to abstain on this issue. Ambassador Lodge is known to have told State Department officials that they had failed to take sufficiently into account certain factors at the UN. "Usually Lodge wins his point. Sometimes the 'instructions' he gets from Washington are verbatim playbacks of what he wrote out himself."[55] Senator John Sparkman, after his service as a delegate to the General Assembly, wrote, "it is not so much a case of the executive department telling the delegation what it shall do on a particular case, as it is a matter of exchange of views, negotiation of any differences that may exist. . . and a coming together of the minds. . ."[56]

This "exchange of views" or "coming together of the minds" is often complicated as policy proposals made at USUN must be referred back to the Department of State for corroboration and all those involved in making the original position need to be consulted anew and their approval secured on any revised policy. Sometimes there is ample time to do this; at other times there is only an hour. With officials already busy with other duties, no interdepartmental committee meeting is possible though all may be canvassed by phone. There are other times when only minutes are available and it is possible only to obtain approval from one or two officials and let them explain the situation later to others. One American representative, faced with an unexpected situation, obtained a 20-minute recess. To obtain his instruction, it was necessary to interrupt a conference between the Assistant Secretary of State-IO and an Am-

---

[55] "United Nations: The Organized Hope," *Time,* Vol. 77, August 11, 1958, p.13.

[56] *Nomination of Philip C. Jessup,* Hearings before a Subcommittee of the Committee on Foreign Relations, U. S. Senate, 82nd Cong., 1st Session, 1951, p.344.

bassador. On another occasion when the Assistant Secretary of State-IO was unavailable, an instruction was secured from an Under-Secretary of State within ten minutes. The story is told of one United States representative who obtained a brief recess at the UN to get new instructions and quickly telephoned the Department only to be told that the Assistant Secretary of State-IO was watching the UN debate on television and could not be interrupted. The necessity for having instructions can be frequently useful to American (and other) delegates at the UN when they do not wish to take a position at that moment. Delegates can honestly say, "I have no instructions on this matter at present. I must consult my government," thereby gaining a day or two in the negotiations. For newcomers to multilateral diplomacy, this tactic can be especially helpful in buying time and preparing sound positions for debate.

In any event, there is a constant two-way flow of information, queries, and suggestions between the Department of State and the mission. In the last half of 1964 USUN received 9,370 telegrams from the Department.[57] Probably no other United States mission has such constant contact with Washington and no other mission to the UN deals so closely with its foreign office as the USUN does with the State Department. This is both an advantage and a hindrance.

In 1958 Senators Hickenlooper and Mansfield, members of the United States delegation to the General Assembly, criticized the machinery available to the mission and the degree of control exercised by the Department:

> We are not, on the basis of our limited experience, in a position to suggest precisely where the line ought to be drawn between firm central control over policy and flexibility in its pursuit at the United Nations. However, many

---

[57] Martin Mayer, " 'The Governor' at Work at the U.N.," *New York Times Magazine,* February 7, 1965, p.86.

of those who have worked day in and day out with other delegations . . . feel that the line as now drawn errs on the side of excessive central control. As a result, it is contended, other delegations are often unnecessarily antagonized or alienated on particular issues and U. S. representatives are frequently handicapped in their efforts to win support for undertakings in which we are interested. . . It is certainly the case that the official position on almost any issue is spelled out by Washington in very minute detail. The delegation is guided very closely not only on questions of substance but often even on matters of procedure.[58]

The senators admitted, however, that this was the practice under which many other delegations to the UN also operated. With respect to the problem of obtaining clearances for proposed policy revisions, they felt:

The requirement would not be so burdensome, perhaps, if only one bureau of the Department of State were involved in sanctioning them. Not infrequently, however, even a slight change in the phrase of a statement of an official position . . . may call for clearance by a number of bureaus and offices scattered through various executive agencies and departments.

Apart from the enormous cost in salaries and time which must be involved in these clearance practices, a desirable change may be so long delayed or so watered down before it is sanctioned by Washington that it loses all or most of its value in New York.

The United States has a highly competent Ambassador and an excellent staff in New York to conduct our business at the United Nations. These men and women appear well versed in the basic policies and positions of the United States and in the intricate requirements of parliamentary leadership and maneuver in the General Assembly. Much might be gained, therefore, if they were permitted a measure of greater flexibility. It should result in savings on costs of policy. It should permit more effective operations at the United Nations. Most important, increased flexibility should enchance the acceptability of our policies and give a greater vitality to our leadership in the United Nations.[59]

---

[58] *Observations on the United Nations,* Report of Senator Bourke B. Hickenlooper and Senator Mike Mansfield, U. S. Senate, 86th Cong., 1st Sess., Senate Doc. No. 26, April 30, 1959, p.7.
[59] *Idem.*

Probably all State Department officials would agree that the mission should have the maximum of flexibility but the criticism that even "a slight change in the phrase of a statement" requires approval in Washington seems overdrawn. Those familiar with international negotiations can point out that such changes are just what often separates success from failure.

5

United States Coordination
of Policy Through the
United Nations

Although the Department of State is central to the formulation of United States foreign policy, it is only one of many American agencies involved in foreign affairs. Some are very importantly and directly concerned with international relations and others less so. All of them keep informed of UN activities in their respective areas of interest and some participate directly in the administration of American policy by sharing in the policy-coordination process already described, by being represented directly at UN meetings, and by implementing international decisions for the United States government. This is particularly important in the case of the UN Specialized Agencies.

The Department of Agriculture, for example, which is primarily interested in FAO, includes the Foreign Agricultural Service, the International Agricultural Development Service, and offices for export programs, barter and stockpiling, and trade, subjects that are represented in a variety of UN activities. Since an important need of the underdeveloped nations is agricultural foods and fibres, the Foreign Agricultural Service and the International Agricultural Development Service work with FAO to help governments develop programs that may, in the long-run, provide sufficient food for their peoples; other agencies in the Department of Agriculture, such as Export Programs, Barter and Stockpiling, the Commodity Credit Corporation, and the Federal Crop Insurance Corporation are concerned with exporting surplus agricultural commodities in the years immediately ahead. The Agricultural Research Service and the Foreign Economics Divisions, meanwhile, are interested in aiding research in various parts of the world through bodies such as FAO and UNESCO, and in sharing in the knowledge obtained from this activity. Likewise the staffs of the Department of Agriculture who deal with cotton, coffee, cocoa, grain, and sugar problems watch every relevant action of the regional economic commissions of ECOSOC: namely, the Economic Commission for Latin America (ECLA), the Economic Commission for Europe (ECE), the Economic Commission for Asia and the Far East (ECAFE), and the Economic Commission for Africa (ECA)—and of FAO.

The Department of Commerce contains a Bureau of International Commerce with divisions to deal with international organizations, foreign business practices, finance, resources, investments, regional economics, trade analysis, and trade promotion; it observes the activities of the Transport and Communications, Fiscal, and Statistical commissions of ECOSOC; the use of GATT; the United Nations Trade and Development Conference (UNCTAD); and the United Nations Industrial Development Organization (UNOID). UNCTAD has particularly stressed expansion of foreign trade for economic development which would vitally affect the commercial policies of the United States and therefore be of central interest to the Department of Commerce.

The Department of Commerce also contains the Bureau of the Census whose work is related to the Population and Statistical Commissions of ECOSOC; the Maritime Administration which works with the Inter-governmental Maritime Consultative Organization (IMCO); the National Bureau of Standards which deals with UNESCO, ICAO, and ITU; the Weather Bureau has relations with WMO, ICAO, and ITU; and the Coast and Geodetic Survey, with the Office of Oceanography, has a direct interest in the work of ITU and WMO. At the 1965 ITU conference in Geneva, for example, one interesting facet of this relationship was examined: much of the world's water surface is virtually unexplored, and there is little knowledge of water and wind conditions. These facts can be registered by automatic electronic devices located on buoys and broadcast from a thousand oceanic spots to a few central stations. The difficulty is that there are not enough wavelengths and the time is rapidly approaching when ITU will have assigned to various governments all the available bands of frequencies. A new device, however, may permit a few wavelengths to cover all these ocean "broadcasting stations" by the use of intermittent broadcasts with a hundred stations using the same frequency at different times.

The Department of Health, Education, and Welfare is similarly involved with many kinds of UN activities: its Food and Drug Administration works with FAO, the Narcotic Drugs Commission of ECOSOC, the Permanent Central Opium Board, and the Drug Supervisory Board; the Office of Education works with UNESCO; the Public Health Service and the National Institutes of Health deal with WHO; the Social Security Administration with

ILO; and the Welfare Administration with the Social Commission of ECOSOC.

Other United States agencies are less obviously related to UN activities. The Department of the Treasury, for example, like every other major executive department (except Interior) has an Assistant Secretary for International Affairs. Under him fall the offices dealing with international monetary, financial, and economic affairs, the balance of payments, financial policy coordinations and operations, gold and foreign exchange operations, and the affairs of Latin America, the industrial nations, and the developing nations. These officials are concerned with the work of the IBRD, IMF, the Special Fund, the International Finance Corporation (IFC), International Development Association (IDA), the regional economic commissions of ECOSOC, GATT, and UNCTAD.

All questions involving UN peacekeeping activities or a permanent UN police force are of obvious interest to the Department of Defense. Questions of disarmament concern not only the Department of Defense but the Arms Control and Disarmament Agency, the Office of Emergency Planning in the Executive Office of the President, the Atomic Energy Commission and the United States Mission to the International Atomic Energy Agency in Vienna, as well as the agencies involved in readjustment in the national economy in the event of any major disarmament, such as the Departments of Agriculture, Commerce, and Labor, and AID. When the General Assembly wrestled with the problem of rival claims to Antarctica and the possible use of this area for hostile action, the Navy and the Air Force, which already had bases there, were concerned, as well as the Department of the Interior since it was reported that several minerals had been discovered in Antarctica, while the Weather Bureau in the Department of Commerce had a continuing interest in weather conditions there.

Since its beginning, the UN has been vitally interested in the development and protection of human rights. The Women's Bureau and the Children's Bureau in the Department of Labor have obvious interests in the rights of these groups; the Educational and Cultural Affairs Office in the Department of State is concerned about cultural rights, the Department of Health, Education, and Welfare with educational rights and welfare problems; the Department of Justice and the Legal Advisor in the Department of State follows the protection of rights for Americans abroad as well as any new statements or definitions of human rights like the Universal Declaration of Human Rights and the proposed Covenants of Human Rights. Moreover, the United States Information Agency seeks to present to other peoples a picture of the place of human rights in the American society and thus needs to be informed of changes anywhere in the world.

The UN has had considerable success with refugees, both in providing for them in refugee camps and in clearing these camps through resettlement projects. The Public Health Service and the National Institutes of Health in the Department of Health, Education, and Welfare have dealt with health problems in the camps and with possible health problems when refugees are admitted to the United States, the Immigration and Naturalization Service in the Department of Justice with legal problems of entry, the Departments of Agriculture and Labor with possible displacement of American workers if large numbers of refugees are permitted to enter the country, the Department of Commerce with goods made by refugees in Hong Kong and exported to the United States, and the Federal Bureau of Investigation with the smuggling of foreign agents into the country in the guise of refugees.

While this discussion has centered around relationships between executive agencies and UN bodies, it should be remembered that it is necessary for these agencies to keep one eye on Congress at all times so that the policies adopted in the executive branch will receive legal and financial support rather than create opposition. The role of Congress in international organizations will be examined in some detail later.

With so many government bodies interested in the topics with which the UN deals, inter-departmental coordinating committees inevitably have sprouted in Washington. By the middle of the 1950's there were twelve that attempted to coordinate policy on aviation, disarmament, food and agriculture, education, human rights, labor, social welfare, narcotics, monetary and financial problems, non-self-governing territories, tele-communications and economic matters. Subsequently the number was drastically reduced, so that by 1965 there were only five: the Inter-departmental Committee on Foreign Policy Relating to Human Rights, the United Nations Economic Committee, the Interdepartmental Committee on Narcotics, the Interdepartmental Committee on International Labor Policy, and the National Advisory Council on International Monetary and Financial Problems.

One of the most active is the United Nations Economic Committee (UNEC) on which are represented the government agencies most concerned with economic problems under discussion in the UN: namely, the departments of State, Commerce, Treasury, Agriculture, Interior, Health, Education, and Welfare, Urban Affairs, as well as AID, the Bureau of the Budget, and the Federal Reserve Board. UNEC is not a drafting but a policy-deciding body, except for minor phrasing changes. The position papers—sometimes as many as 20 or 30 for a single meeting— are written in one of the member-agencies, or sometimes different parts are written in different agencies, and they are brought to UNEC to establish United States policy whenever an international economic conference is scheduled. Any member-agency can

claim *primary clearance,* which means that it has a
chance to examine the document, or part of it, prior to
consideration by UNEC. It is recognized that the Department of State has the final authority to resolve policy
questions, but one official observed that he could re-
member no occasion when the representatives on UNEC
failed to settle a disputed matter. The individuals at-
tending UNEC meetings are senior officers, normally
GS-15 or higher, which means that they have had years
of experience in dealing with policy matters, but there is
a lack of continuity in UNEC itself since most officers are
reassigned after approximately two years of service with
the Committee.

The National Advisory Council on International
Monetary and Financial Problems (NAC) is also very
important in coordinating international policy as a
statutory interdepartmental body, having been created
in the Bretton Woods Agreements Act of 1945. By law,
the members of NAC are the Secretaries of the Treasury,
State, and Commerce, the Chairman of the Board of
Governors of the Federal Reserve System, and the President and Chairman of the Board of Directors of the Ex-
port-Import Bank. These officials are often represented
by their deputies at NAC meetings. Participating regularly in the work of NAC are the United States Executive
Director of IMF; the Executive Directors of IBRD, IDA,
and IFC; the Executive Director of the Inter-American
Development Bank; and representatives of the Department of Agriculture and the Bureau of the Budget. NAC
has a staff committee which meets frequently, doing the
staff work and preparing the position papers for NAC
consideration. NAC decisions are particularly important
to the work of the IBRD and its affiliates as well as the
IMF where, since votes are related to quotas, the United
States has the largest voice. One official of the Treasury
Department was loathe to balance the influence of the

Treasury Department on NAC decisions against the influence of other agencies such as the Department of State; but he acknowledged that the Treasury plays an extremely important role. As in UNEC, decisions in NAC are normally made by consensus rather than by vote. Because of its statutory basis and the nature of its work, NAC recommendations frequently necessitate subsequent Congressional action. In 1962, for example, Congress authorized United States participation in special IMF borrowing arrangements through loans not to exceed two billion dollars, and in 1963 it authorized an increase of one billion dollars in the capital stock of IBRD. Because of the importance of the American government in international monetary and economic matters, the work of NAC plays a very significant, if largely unheralded, role in American relations with certain UN bodies.

Since so many agencies in Washington participate in the formulation of policy on matters involving the UN, representatives of these agencies frequently are included in delegations to international conferences; indeed, in some cases, no member of an international delegation comes from the Department of State. This is particularly true when conferences are small and deal with technical matters. At one recent meeting of the Subcommittee on Mineral Resources Development of the ECAFE, for example, the single American representative was a specialist from the Bureau of Mines in the Department of the Interior, although his advisers came from the Foreign Service.

In a large conference, even one which deals with technical matters, the American delegation normally represents both the State Department and the government agencies that have a principal interest in the subject-matter of the conference. At the 1958 UN Conference on the Law of the Sea, for example, the head of the

United States delegation was a Special Assistant to the Under Secretary of State while the other delegates consisted of a Vice Admiral from the Department of the Navy, the Commissioner of the Fish and Wildlife Service of the Department of the Interior, and two Assistant Legal Advisers from the Department of State. One member of the United States Senate was included as congressional adviser. Attached to the delegation was a sizable group of advisers, representing both government agencies and non-governmental groups throughout the country. The government advisers came from the Geological Survey of the Department of the Interior, the Federal Communications Commission, the Office of the Secretary of Defense, the Legal Advisor of the Department of State, the Admiralty Section of the Department of Justice, the Atomic Energy Commission, the Chief of Naval Operations and Judge Advocate General of the Department of the Navy, the Office of Transport and Communications of the Department of State, the Fish and Wildlife Service of the Department of the Interior, the United States Coast Guard, the Geographer of the Department of State, the Maritime Administration of the Department of Commerce, and the offices of European Affairs, Far Eastern Affairs, and Inter-American Affairs of the Department of State. The non-governmental advisers came from the International North Pacific Fisheries Commission, the American Tunaboat Association, the Western Union Telegraph Co., the National Shrimp Congress, and the National Canners Association. At such a conference, the representatives from the Department of State obviously do not have complete voice on policy matters, although the Department may have to decide which of the competing views are to be amalgamated into the official policy.

An appropriate way to conclude this discussion of the close relationship between a large number of executive agencies and UN bodies is to refer to the designation by the UN of 1965 as International Cooperation Year (ICY) , a time when national governments would place special emphasis on the many kinds of international cooperation currently in existence. In November 1964 President Lyndon Johnson named a Cabinet committee to coordinate American participation in the ICY, and it eventually included representatives from the departments of Agriculture, Commerce, Defense, Health, Education and Welfare, Interior, Labor, Post Office, State, and Treasury; AID, AEC, Federal Aviation Agency, Federal Communications Commission, Attorney General, National Aeronautics and Space Administration, National Science Foundation, Peace Corps, United States Information Agency, and the United States Mission to the UN, with the Assistant Secretary of State for International Organization Affairs as chairman.

The preparation of American policy for presentation in the UN tends to be a cumbersome process, involving the coordination of a wide variety of executive agencies and bringing together special interests and viewpoints until the policy becomes, as nearly as possible, one for the United States as a whole rather than that of any of the competing groups.

6

The United States
Congress and the
United Nations

Under the American Constitution the President is the
Chief of State and the sole organ of communication with
foreign governments. But the Congress is not without
power in matters that affect international relations, especially in appropriations, and the Senate must advise
and consent to the ratification of any treaty.

The United Nations Charter and all amendments to it
are treaties. Thus, the question of holding a conference
to review the Charter and consider amendments was
carefully considered by the Senate Foreign Relations
Committee in 1955. With the General Assembly's passage of two amendments to the Charter in December
1963, increasing the size of the Security Council and
ECOSOC, the question of amendments formally came

before the Senate for the first time. The United States failed to take any action on these amendments for eighteen months and only ratified them just before the convening of the 20th General Assembly in September 1965. This was the deadline established by the General Assembly for ratification and the United States was not only the ninety-fourth member of the UN to do so, but the last of the Big Five whose approval is required under the provisions of Article 108 of the Charter. Moreover, the United States up to 1966 had failed to act favorably on the Genocide Convention and three Human Rights Conventions.

Congress is obligated by treaty to appropriate money for the American share of the regular UN budget, but not for voluntary contributions to UN agencies and programs. No American delegate can commit his government in advance in such cases, although, because of the United States fiscal year, half of the UN year is usually completed before Congress makes funds available for these programs. This has frequently been awkward, as in the case of the UN Bond issue in 1962. As in other parts of the United States-UN relationship, the failure of some legislators to understand UN problems has led to uncertainty and misunderstanding.

Almost every aspect of modern legislative jurisdiction relates to problems that involve the UN and more than half of the standing legislative committees deal regularly with problems of international significance. UN agencies are concerned with American policy on defense, general welfare, foreign commerce, naturalization, almost all of the powers of Congress as listed in Article 1 of the Constitution.

On occasion, Congress has taken the initiative and determined American policy towards the UN. Thus, in 1947 when Congress was considering the Truman proposal for aid to Greece and Turkey, some members were sensitive to the criticism that American policy might bypass the UN. Senator Arthur Vanderberg and others amended the President's program to direct the withdrawal of all aid whenever the General Assembly or the Security Council decided that such assistance was no longer necessary or desirable. On another occasion, Congress objected to certain aspects of the use of the funds provided for the United Nations International Children's Emergency Fund (UNICEF) and essentially cut off all American contributions until changes were made. Although the United States faced the charge that it did not care what happened to the colored children of the world and although the General Assembly approved the continuation of UNICEF as it had been, a few months later the organization was changed to accord with practically everything that the American Congress desired.

Indeed, Congressional power is not restricted to the field of legislation. Congress has the right to voice its views by resolutions. No one has questioned the power of Congress to use this method to oppose the admission of the People's Republic of China to the UN. Congress passed resolutions in 1951 to support an American demand in the General Assembly that Red China be condemned as an aggressor, and this pressure contributed to action by the Assembly. But when Congress in 1953 tried to tell the UN that the United States would not contribute to the UN budget if China was admitted, the President intervened.

The House Foreign Affairs Committee and the Senate Foreign Relations Committee have established a number of sub-committees to deal with specific geographic areas and topics, including international organizations. These subcommittees, although used mostly for consultation rather than legislative work, have proved helpful in maintaining a feeling of bipartisan effort and executive-legislative teamwork. Approximately thirty staff experts who work entirely on foreign affairs, are attached to the two foreign relations committees and to the Legislative Reference Service, and they assist members of Congress materially in examining and understanding problems that arise in the UN. Moreover, the office of the Assistant Secretary of State for Congressional Relations includes one staff member who specializes in international organization affairs.

Influential members of Congress, of course, are constantly consulted by the President on all matters seriously involving American foreign relations. Often the Chief Executive may inform Congressional leaders of his intentions, to gain a reaction or win consensus. Sometimes, as when Senator J. W. Fulbright, Chairman of the Senate Foreign Relations Committee was asked to attend the meeting at the State Department 4 April 1961 during the Cuban crisis, they may actually participate in the decision-making process.

Congress and Delegations to the UN

Having in mind the fate of the Versailles Treaty in the Senate and the need for support of the Administration in the legislature on international matters, Presidents have been careful to include members of Congress in delegations to UN meetings, starting with the San Francisco Conference in 1945. Since 1951 it has been customary to include two members of Congress among the delegates to the General Assembly, two from the House of Representatives in odd-numbered years when the members do not face elections, and two from the Senate in even-numbered years. Almost always, they have been members of the foreign affairs committees. Congressmen have also attended many other UN meetings, either as delegates or as advisers. Some members have not only been consulted on UN aspects of foreign relations, but have directly participated in their formulation.

This system has instructed many members of Congress on UN procedures and problems. Senator Vandenberg, who changed his attitude considerably on international matters, in his participation in the San Francisco Conference in 1945 came to grips with many international organization problems for the first time. Representatives Frances Bolton and James Richards were sobered to find "that our motives and even our integrity were being challenged."[60] Congressman Walter Judd is said to have changed his attitude towards the United Nations Technical Assistance Program after his service at the General Assembly in 1957.

At the same time, Congressmen have frequently been able to inform foreign delegates to the UN about American public opinion. In November 1951, for example, Vyshinsky complained that the Mutual Security Act was an aggressive action by the American government. As members of the House Foreign Affairs Committee which had considered this legislation, Representatives Mike Mansfield and John Vorys were in a splendid position to reply to the Soviet charge; indeed, Mansfield was so successful in his defense of American policy that President Truman personally asked him to return to the second part of the General Assembly session in Paris despite Mansfield's plans to remain in Washington for the opening of Congress. Meanwhile Vorys, assigned to the less dramatic 5th Committee (Administrative and Budgetary) where he worked hard for a reduction of the American assessment to the UN budget, startled the committee one day by asking, "Who picks up the check?" He asked the question five times, using the five official languages

[60] *Report on the 8th Session of the General Assembly of the United Nations,* by Hon. Frances P. Bolton and Hon. James P. Richards... 83rd Cong., 2d Sess., Union Calendar No. 626, House Report No. 1695, May 28, 1954, p.7.

of the organization, and then concluded that the question had a sad sound in any language.[61] This legislator's approach to the problem scored an effective point for the American position. Most of the Congressional delegates have taken their duties at the UN very seriously and have rendered a positive service for their government.[62] As delegates, Congressmen temporarily become a part of the executive branch technically acting under instructions of the President, and thus have an anomalous position under the United States Constitution, but there has been no serious objection to this usage. A suggestion that the members of Congress be "advisers" rather than "delegates" has not attracted much support and the present system seems likely to continue.

As members of the UN delegations, however, the members of Congress have hardly been pawns of the Administration and frequently have registered their dissent with State Department policy. In particular, they have commented on relations between Washington and USUN.

In 1960 Senators Aiken and Morse were delegates to the General Assembly. In addition to the customary joint report, each wrote a separate supplementary report. Morse devoted almost all of the thirty-three pages of text to the "headquarters-field" relationship:

> We, in turn, owed a duty to the State Department and through it, to the White House, to register our respectful dissents, reservations, and suggestions for changes . . . whenever we became convinced that the realities and facts which we faced on the United Nations firing line could not be

---

[61] *New York Times,* December 11, 1951, p.23.

[62] Mrs. Roosevelt has noted, however, the case of one Senator who never arrived in time to read his documents. He would arrive for a briefing, breathless and with little or no knowledge of the matter under discussion. "I sometimes lectured him about doing his homework, but there was never any improvement." (Roosevelt, *op. cit.,* p.92.)

squared with the instructions which Washington had sent us. Surprisingly enough, this happened rather frequently.[63]

Morse was assigned to the Fourth, or Trusteeship, Committee and was responsible for presenting the American government's views on two items, the general question of colonialism and the South West African problem. On both of these matters, he disagreed almost completely with the instructions provided. On a proposal to send a sub-committee of the General Assembly to report on conditions in South West Africa Morse wrote,

> I could not believe my own ears when the Assistant Secretary of State told me over the long-distance telephone that his lawyers believed that the proposal was in violation of the League of Nations mandate over South West Africa. I laughingly told the Assistant Secretary of State that if his lawyers had given him that advice, he ought to send them back to law school. He then argued that the final resolution might be construed as United Nations interference in the contentious case filed before the World Court . . . My reply . . . was that if he and his lawyers would read the record of the debate before the Fourth Committee, they would see that the final resolution had been drafted to meet that very objection. . .[64]

Despite the forcefulness of his feelings, Senator Morse did not succeed in obtaining Department approval for what he wanted, though the Department did authorize an abstention instead of a "no" vote.

Congress is probably more active in the field of foreign affairs now than ever before. The executive and legislative branches of government have learned how to work together better, and are more aware that the interests of the United States are best advanced when they do so. Each respects the other's power, but both seek to maintain their own share of national responsibility.

---

[63] *The United States in the United Nations, 1960, A Turning Point.* Supplementary Report to the Committee on Foreign Relations by Sen. Wayne Morse, U. S. Senate, 87th Cong., 1st Sess., Feb., 1961, p.2.

[64] *Ibid.*, pp.14-15.

7

Future United States– United Nations Relationships

The attitudes of the United States government and the American people toward the UN have been and will continue to be in a state of flux. Since 1964 the conflict over assessments for UN peacekeeping operations and the question of applying Article 19 to the Soviet bloc and other states, which completely stymied the 19th General Assembly, have certainly influenced the American perspective of the UN. Despite a diplomatic defeat, the United States, through Ambassador Arthur Goldberg, has declared its policy to be unchanged:

> Our views on these matters have not represented a bargaining position, nor have they changed. They have not been based on narrow national interest, but on the clear language of the Charter and what seemed to us to be the clear interests of the Organization. . . .
>
> We . . . cannot abandon our adherence to positions which we firmly believe to be constitutionally, legally, procedurally, and administratively correct.

> Much less can we abandon positions taken and precedents established by the Assembly itself by overwhelming majorities, acting within the framework of the Charter and according to its established procedures.[65]

No government wanted to be held responsible for continuing the UN stalemate of 1964 and the possible collapse of the General Assembly. Consequently, there was an agreement for a *modus vivendi* to permit the Assembly to proceed with its business, although no government has technically surrendered its position. There has been no decision, only a truce, and members of the UN have discovered that they can live with truces for years.

What are the results of this truce on American attitudes towards the UN? There is certainly no reason to expect American withdrawal from the UN. Even at extreme moments in 1965 there was no official hint or threat of such action. Shrill American voices have often called for withdrawal from the UN, but such cries have never had any large audience in the United States. A consideration of withdrawal might arise if the People's Republic of China were admitted to the UN in the near future. While the Department of State may be braced against an adverse vote on the question of Chinese representation, it is not clear that Congress would be equally prepared or acquiescent. If, in such a case, the anguished cries of ultra-conservatives in the United States were mingled with the outraged demands of any sizable group of legislators, the President might have to reconsider policy towards the UN. But this appears to be the only situation in the near future in which the United States might reconsider its membership in the UN.

A more likely event is a reduction of American enthusiasm and support—particularly financial—for the UN and its activities. The Article 19 controversy caused

---

[65] *USUN Press Release No. 4615,* August 16, 1965, pp.2-3.

widespread dissatisfaction for the first time with a UN decision in the United States. Much of the American enthusiasm for the UN has been idealistic, but what will happen to this popular enthusiasm, given a "defeat" on an issue where the position of the government seems entirely "just" and "proper" is uncertain. Widespread apathy towards the UN could develop and public opinion in the United States might resemble that in certain European countries towards the League of Nations during the inter-war years: governments maintained membership at Geneva but paid little attention to the League in their diplomatic relations while the public was almost wholly apathetic or cynical.

The matter of public support will, of course, affect financial support of the UN by the American government. While the Department of State sees general advantages to the United States in continued membership and contributions, Congress may become more critical. Many Congressmen have already denounced the liberality of American financial contributions in recent years and this view has been strengthened since the Article 19 controversy.

Ambassador Goldberg emphasized the gravity of this in his statement on 16 August 1965 when he said:

> . . . if any member can insist on making an exception to the principle of collective financial responsibility with respect to certain activities of the Organization, the United States reserves the same option to make exceptions if, in our view, strong and compelling reasons exist for doing so. There can be no double standard among the members of the Organization.[66]

Such a view could become a new American policy on the financing of the UN, a policy of allowing other members to pay the bills—at least outside of the regular UN budget—or forego the benefits of the programs.

---

[66] *Ibid.*, p.4.

The President would surely be reluctant to accept such a policy, since it would feed anti-American propaganda abroad and since the Administration believes these programs are constructive adjuncts of economic and social development. An increasing portion of UN activities centers around technical assistance and the services of the Specialized Agencies. The United States can hardly afford to abandon the UN technical assistance program without antagonizing the many undeveloped states of the UN whose support it will need on political matters— tomorrow and in the years ahead.

Having committed so much to the UN in the past twenty years, it hardly seems likely that the United States would let the organization drift with the international winds and currents. The United States has been singularly successful in the past in having the General Assembly approve policies which the United States has favored. Rarely has the General Assembly approved policies to which the United States was opposed. Conditions have changed. It is now possible to achieve a two-thirds majority in the Assembly with a group of members representing only 10% of the population of UN members, and only 5% of the contributions to the regular UN budget. A UNESCO conference in 1965 voted a budget by a large numerical majority although the states voting affirmatively represented only 30% of the budget contributions. And Washington was seriously concerned about the tendency of the less developed countries to vote majority recommendations at the 1964 UNCTAD conference in Geneva over the opposition of the minority members who were expected to finance and implement such recommendations.

Nevertheless, the General Assembly has never yet recommended a peacekeeping operation against the opposition of the United States. All sense of political reality will not be lost just because it is theoretically possible to put together an anti-United States vote. In fact, the votes of the small states are frequently divided. In 1953, for example, just after the vote on Indian participation in the proposed political conference on Korea, one Latin American delegate reported that some of his colleagues who voted with the United States "would have preferred to see India invited but they felt that the dominant consideration was not to let the United States go down to defeat on a major political issue."[67] Such feelings have not evaporated even in the larger composition of the General Assembly today. In April 1965 a Deputy Assistant Secretary of State-IO went so far as to say that "the United States has been prepared to take whatever risks are inherent in the principle that voluntary peacekeeping operations may be initiated or financed by the General Assembly free from great-power veto because we recognize a long-term interest in developing this means of containing violence in the nuclear age."[68] In confronting the problem of voting majorities in the General Assembly, the American government decided that the risks are bearable and that its diplomats can find ways of maintaining balance in the UN and advancing United States foreign policy.

American leadership in the UN has led to many contributions both in peacekeeping and in economic and social programs. The imagination of American officials to catalyze the UN should be equal to present problems, although they have often been criticized for having devoted so much of their energies to opposing rather than creating UN action.

In the realm of peacekeeping the UN may offer important benefits to the United States, despite the new

---

[67] *New York Times,* August 28, 1953, p.3.

[68] Gardner, Richard N. "United Nations Procedures and Power Realities: The International Apportionment Problem," *Department of State Bulletin,* vol. 52 No. 350, May 10, 1965, p.705.

membership and the financial difficulties. The Cuban missile crisis of 1962, more than any other political conflict in years, could have provoked the United States to act unilaterally without the encumbrances of multilateral diplomacy. Once its basic policy decision was made, however, the United States found the UN to be a most useful diplomatic machine. Ambassador Stevenson could have sought no finer stage on which to play his drama of indicting the Soviet Union before the whole world than in the halls of the UN. The United States could have found no more cooperative referee than the Secretary General in his pleas for détente. No American could have said or done anything more useful to his government than when the UN made an offer of impartial inspection, only to be refused by the Cuban leader. If the American officials had written the script, they could have asked for no better demonstration of which state really threatened the peace of the world.

John D. Hickerson, a former Assistant Secretary of State for United Nations Affairs, many years ago suggested the basis of successful leadership by the United States in the UN: the positions taken by Washington should be "sound and morally right" and truly representative of the American public; there must be a true partnership with allies, through advance consultation and whatever concessions are necessary; and "We must be able to persuade them of the essential correctness of our position . . . we must understand their doubts and answer them . . . in terms of their own self-interests. . . . We must seek to lead and not to dominate."[69] These conditions of leadership still obtain. Will the American government and people accept the fact that they cannot have all they want in the UN and are they prepared to act accordingly?

---

[69] Hickerson, John D., "Problems Facing the 7th General Assembly," *Department of State Bulletin,* vol. 27, October 27, 1952, p.649.

Have they enough patience and understanding to weather reverses and uncertainties in the UN and still not lose sight of the high-minded goals for the future? That, in short, is the challenge to American leadership in the UN.

The United States government has another problem with respect to foreign affairs and the UN which may be harder to solve, namely the ability of Washington to coordinate its own agencies so that it can provide leadership that will be trusted by those countries whose support America needs. All of the officials of the American government who need to participate in the making of policy for presentation in the UN should have an opportunity to do so, but decision-making cannot be so delayed and diluted that the results are hardly worth the effort expended. Internally, the conduct of foreign policy in the American government has progressed a long way since the beginning of the UN. Senator Henry M. Jackson has referred to the fact that "not until the end of 1950, when General Marshall was Secretary of Defense, had the Secretary of State with his senior aides, ever sat down with the Secretary of Defense and the Chiefs of Staff to take counsel on a common problem. . ."[70] Meanwhile the United States had been trying to repulse North Korean aggression for almost six months and the two government departments most directly involved in the effort in Korea were not in high level, constant collaboration.

Since then weekly inter-departmental meetings in Washington have been instituted, and the old situation no longer exists. But the problem of coordination in American government has not been solved by any means. An interesting gap in the present administrative structure

---

[70] *Hearings* Before the Subcommittee on National Security and International Operations of the Committee on Government Operations, U. S. Senate, 89th Cong., 1st Sess., July 27, 1965, p.186.

in Washington was revealed in 1965 in an exchange between Senator Ribicoff and William McC.Martin, Jr., Chairman of the Board of Governors of the Federal Reserve System:

> Sen. Ribicoff. . . . When the Secretary of State makes a foreign policy decision do they ever consult with you as to its impact on America's international monetary position . . . or do they make the decision and let you catch up with them?

> Mr. Martin. I think it is fair to say we usually catch up with them. . . .

> Sen. Ribicoff. . . . don't you think that the State Department does not have the right to make these decisions in a vacuum and allow the entire apparatus of Government . . . to try to catch up. . . . ?

> Mr. Martin. Yes; I agree with that. I am a member of the National Advisory Council . . . and we made this point frequently through the Secretary of the Treasury.[71]

On 15 March 1966 President Lyndon Johnson, faced with a situation in which some federal government agencies made decisions on foreign affairs without clearing them with the Department of State, issued a memorandum which explicitly assigned to the Secretary of State the task of coordinating all participation in international organizations by the American government. Coordination, obviously, was still a problem.

This lack of coordination in the United States government can have grave consequences for United States relations with the UN. On 15 April 1961 just prior to the invasion of the Bay of Pigs, there was an air strike against Cuba that originated in Nicaragua. When the Cuban foreign minister moved to convene an emergency meeting of the First Committee of the General Assembly, the Assistant Secretary of State for International Organization Affairs in Washington tried to ascertain the

---

[71] *Ibid.*, Part 4, August 30, 1965, p.202.

facts by calling the Bureau of Inter-American Affairs in the State Department which in turn called the Central Intelligence Agency. This Agency "promptly and definitely" asserted that the air strike was the work of defectors from Castro's air force. The Assistant Secretary passed this information on to Ambassador Adlai Stevenson at the UN who presented parts of the Agency's "cover story" in the UN meeting. It soon became apparent that this "cover story" was breaking down and that Stevenson "had been permitted to misinform the UN. Stevenson was understandably indignant. Rusk was remorseful."[72]

The UN, of course, is only one channel of American foreign policy. The delegation and mission in New York watch "their area" and judge events and policies by their effect in the UN, while officials in Washington must take the whole world picture into consideration. But if the United States is to present a reputable argument in the UN, the responsible officials there must know and understand their government's policy. They must be able to present it with confidence so that other delegates to the UN can accept it.

The problem of cooperation and comprehension exists both between the United States and the UN and within the American government itself. The United States can control only certain aspects of the former, but it has sole control over the latter. While the obstacles to a coordinated policy within the United States government are admittedly great, nevertheless Washington must strive to channel all its efforts into one concerted effort in international relations in order to maximize its influence in UN affairs.

The lesson of this study may be that when the United States joined the UN and committed itself to multilateral diplomacy, it assumed complications in foreign relations

[72] Schlesinger, *op. cit.,* p.70.

far beyond the expectations of its most internationally-minded citizens and leaders. While the American government has earnestly shouldered many consequent international responsibilities, it has not yet found its way through this dense diplomatic forest. The new and greater challenges of multilateral diplomacy that lie ahead will call for the best American talents of organization, management, and negotiation to strengthen and expand the work of the UN for world peace and prosperity.

Appendices

APPENDIX ONE

U.S. CONTRIBUTIONS TO INTERNATIONAL ORGANIZATIONS

Source: Subcommittee of the Committee on Appropriations, House of Representatives, 89th Congress, Second Session, Department of State, Washington, 1966.

[In thousands of dollars]

	1965 actual	1966 estimate	1967 estimate
Program by activities:			
United Nations and specialized agencies:			
1. United Nations	$31,256	$33,531	$32,793
2. United Nations Educational, Scientific, and Cultural Organization	5,806	6,882	7,196
3. International Civil Aviation Organization	2,596	2,750	3,208
4. World Health Organization	10,852	12,327	13,722
5. Food and Agriculture Organization	4,102	5,688	7,601
6. International Labor Organization	4,097	4,671	5,085
7. International Telecommunication Union	425	500	515
8. World Meteorological Organization	343	408	520
9. Intergovernmental Maritime Consultative Organization	84	109	136
Subtotal	$59,561	$66,866	$70,776

	1965 actual	1966 estimate	1967 estimate
Programs by activities — Continued			
Inter-American organizations:			
1. Inter-American Indian Institute	$ 62	$ 62	$ 62
2. Inter-American Institute of Agricultural Sciences	1,324	1,549	1,752
3. Pan American Institute of Geography and History	50	50	50
4. Pan American Railway Congress Association	5	5	5
5. Pan American Health Organization	4,263	4,679	5,234
6. Organization of American States	9,809	10,406	10,957
Subtotal	15,573	16,751	18,060
Regional organizations:			
1. South Pacific Commission	140	150	170
2. North Atlantic Treaty Organization	3,454	3,764	3,928
3. North Atlantic Treaty Organization Parliamentary Conference	35	49	54
4. Southeast Asia Treaty Organization	280	579	311
5. Colombo Plan Council for Technical Cooperation	6	7	7
6. Organization for Economic Cooperation and Development	4,404	4,286	4,235
7. International Control Commission for Laos	1,366	422	394
Subtotal	$ 9,085	$ 9,257	$ 9,099

104

APPENDIX ONE (continued)

	1965 actual	1966 estimate	1967 estimate
Other international organizations:			
1. Interparliamentary Union	$ 23	$ 23	$ 23
2. International Bureau of the Permanent Court of Arbitration	1	1	1
3. International Bureau for the Protection of Industrial Property	10	10	10
4. International Bureau for the Publication of Customs Tariffs	9	9	9
5. International Bureau of Weights and Measures	30	42	52
6. International Council of Scientific Unions	65	78	84
7. International Hydrographic Bureau	10	10	10
8. International Sugar Council	16	16	—
9. International Wheat Council	23	23	23
10. International Coffee Organization	139	142	149
11. International Institute for the Unification of Private Law	1	2	2
12. Hague Conference on Private International Law	8	10	8
13. International Atomic Energy Agency	2,238	2,338	2,520
Subtotal	$ 2,573	$ 2,704	$ 2,891
Total obligations	$87,392	$95,578	$100,826

105

APPENDIX TWO

PROPOSED VOLUNTARY CONTRIBUTIONS TO INTERNATIONAL ORGANIZATIONS AND PROGRAMS, FISCAL YEAR 1967

Source: *Foreign Assistance and Related Agencies Appropriation Bill, 1967*, 89th Congress, House of Representatives, **Report No. 2045, 16 September, 1966.**

[In thousands of dollars]

	Ch. 3 (foreign assistance)	Public Law 480 or successor	Other
UN development program	$ 70,000	——	——
UN children's fund	12,000	$ 4,000	——
Indus Basin development fund	33,000	1,000	——
UN technical and operational assistance to the Congo	5,000	——	——
UN/FAO world food program	2,000	25,000	——
IAEA operational program	1,000	——	——
International secretariat for voluntary service	¹165	——	²$ 35
UN emergency force	6,838	——	——
UN relief and works agency	14,000	8,900	——
UN institute for training and research	500	——	——
WHO, medical research	150	——	——
Total	$144,553	$38,900	$ 35

¹ Proposed contribution for calendar year 1967.
² Estimate of personnel costs (3 persons) detailed by Peace Corps to ISVS for last half of fiscal year 1967 (first half of calendar year 1967).

The Committee recommends the appropriation of $140,433,000, the budget estimate. This is a decrease of $4,322,00 below the 1966 appropriation.

In addition, the Committee recommends the approval of $1,000,000 of unobligated funds estimated to be available as of June 30, 1966, to provide additional funds to the UN Children's Fund. This appropriation is authorized by Sec. 302 (b) of the recently passed authorization bill.

107

Index